HOW GOD DELIVERS THE DESPERATE AND HEALS THE HOPELESS

BROKEN
CHAINS

*Finding Peace for
the Raging Soul*

DOUG BATCHELOR

BROKEN CHAINS

Other books by Doug Batchelor:
At Jesus' Feet: The Gospel According to Mary Magdalene
The Richest Caveman
To See the King

BROKEN
CHAINS

Finding Peace for the Raging Soul

DOUG BATCHELOR

Pacific Press® Publishing Association
Nampa, Idaho
Oshawa, Ontario, Canada
www.pacificpress.com

Edited by: Anthony Lester
Cover design: Justinen Creative Group ©
Inside design: Steve Lanto

Copyright © 2004 by
Pacific Press® Publishing Association and Mountain Ministry
Printed in United States of America
All rights reserved

Unless otherwise noted all scriptures are taken from
the NKJV, The New King James Version. Copyright © 1979,
1980, 1982 by Thomas Nelson Inc. Used by permission.
All rights reserved. Texts credited to the KJV are
taken from the King James Version.

Additional copies of this book are available
by calling toll free 1-800-765-6955 or
by visiting http://www.adventistbookcenter.com

[Library of Congress CIP]

ISBN: 0-8163-2042-X

04 05 06 07 08 • 5 4 3 2 1

Table of Contents

Preface

They were considered the most *unlikely* to succeed.

"Don't invite David to the feast; he's just a young minstrel, a shepherd." Yet he was chosen the king of Israel. "Joseph is such an annoying daydreamer; let's kill him or sell him as a slave." Yet he became the prime minister of Egypt. Peter exclaimed, "Depart from me, Lord. I am a sinful man." He was right, yet Jesus said, "Do not be afraid. From now on you will catch men." "Don't associate with Mary; she has a bad reputation." Yet she was chosen to be the first to touch and proclaim the risen Lord.

Have you ever felt that your spiritual condition was stagnant? Or that your hope for future growth was bleak? Have you ever reached the brink of despair, feeling that your personality flaws, bad habits, and selfishness have placed you beyond the reach of redemption?

Then this book is for you . . . and it is for me.

This book is founded on the Gospel account of Jesus' deliverance and total transformation of a man who was possessed by myriad demons. It is the story of a man as far from God as anyone could imagine. His home was a tomb. His only companions were pigs. His only food their leftovers. His only clothes the remnants of chains. And his deranged thoughts were imprisoned within the domain of demons. Not even Hollywood could conjure up a more complete picture of the ultimate hopeless man. He would certainly have won everyone's vote as the most unlikely to succeed.

But then he met Jesus, who cleaned him, clothed him, and commissioned him. In Jesus, his raging heart found rest.

I must admit that I wrote this book, in part, because I have repeatedly found myself returning to this fascinating tale of ultimate deliverance for my own encouragement and inspiration. Because, you see, in a sense, I was that man!

Back in 1973, I was living in a cave high up in the remote desert mountains of Southern California. I too was running around naked, digging for food in supermarket dumpsters, and utterly enslaved by a life of drugs, deceit, immorality, and basic spiritual confusion.* My life was a big "zero." Like the demoniac of Decapolis, I could easily have been nominated the most unlikely to succeed.

---

*Doug Batchelor's personal testimony, *The Richest Caveman*, can be purchased through Mountain Ministry, 5431 Auburn Blvd., Suite A-1, Sacramento, CA 95841. Phone: 916-332-5800

But I found a Bible that somebody left in my cave, and in that Bible I met Jesus.

"Not many wise according to the flesh, not many mighty, not many noble, are called. But God has chosen the foolish things of the world to put to shame the wise, and God has chosen the weak things of the world to put to shame the things which are mighty; and the base things of the world and the things which are despised God has chosen, and the things which are not, to bring to nothing the things that are, that no flesh should glory in His presence."—1 Corinthians 1:26-29, NKJV

God bless you,

Doug Batchelor

The Story of the Demoniac

(Based on Mark 5:1-20 and Luke 8:26-40.)

Jesus crossed the angry waves to make a madman whole.
He who stilled the stormy sea can calm a raging soul.

Through the Storm

It was so quiet that you could hear every tiny wave splash against the boat and every creak of the oars as the disciples took turns rhythmically rowing across the placid waters of Galilee. How vastly different from the howling conditions they weathered only an hour earlier.

When they first embarked on their journey across the lake, the perfectly serene sunset promised them a gentle journey. The light southern breeze meant they could raise the sail, sparing them the arduous task of rowing. But about three miles into the voyage, at the very midpoint of their crossing, things changed rapidly.

BROKEN CHAINS

The light wind changed its direction, now sweeping down from the mountains of Lebanon in the northwest. The sky also grew ominously dark with thickening rolling clouds that thundered their fury. Suddenly, the wind burgeoned into a howling gale with such speed that the men hastily lowered the sail for fear that it might tear—or, worse yet, that they might capsize!

In the frightening tempest, the waves grew ever larger, as if some diabolical power was forcing them up from the deep right before the disciples' eyes. Soon the walls of water began to break over the sides of their modest vessel, extinguishing their flickering lamp and threatening to swamp and sink the floundering craft. The disciples frantically groped for their small leather buckets to begin bailing, but the swirling water rose too fast.

Soon these experienced sailors realized that their efforts would be futile. They recognized that without divine intervention, their situation was hopeless.

Absorbed in their struggles to save themselves, they had all but forgotten Jesus, who was on board with them. Finally remembering their Lord in their helplessness and despair, they cried out, "Master! Master!" But the dense darkness hid Him from their sight, and the roaring tempest drowned out their voices. Had He been washed overboard? Were they now all alone?

Again they called, but their only answer was the shrieking of an angry blast. Their boat was sinking. At any moment, hungry, unforgiving waters would swallow them up.

Then came a superheated flash of lightning, and they saw Him—curled up on a cushion near the stern. Even as frigid water sloshed about Him, Jesus was sleeping soundly through the howling storm.

Why was He sleeping? Perhaps He was so totally exhausted from the ceaseless ministry of the day that even the horrific chaos plaguing the boat did not rouse Him. Whatever the case, the disciples shook Jesus awake, shouting in amazement and despair, "Master, don't you care that we are perishing?"

Jesus calmly sat up. It took only a moment for Him to assess the situation. Then, as the tempest still raged around Him and the waves crashed into the boat, Jesus stood to face the storm. Placing one hand on the mast to steady Himself, He lifted His other hand to the heavens as He had done so often when performing His deeds of mercy. As lightning flashed across the sky and illuminated His peaceful countenance, He spoke boldly to the angry sea.

"Peace, be still."

As the last syllable left His lips, the storm ceased. The angry waves flattened. The dark clouds rolled away, revealing a diamond-studded sky. And the boat rested upon a serene, glassy sea.

Turning to His disciples, Jesus sadly rebuked them. "Why are you so fearful? How is it that you have no faith?" (Mark 4:40).

In the dark, James methodically bailed the remaining water from the lowest point of the craft. Others rowed, rhythmically again, now that the storm was over. They all worked in a numb silence caused by a combination of fatigue, confusion, and awe—but mostly fear. They each wondered, *What kind of man is this, One so unpretentious, yet who can speak and instantly transform a sea of madness into a sea of tranquility?* Not only had He been perfectly calm in what could have been a lethal storm, but He had calmed the storm itself! Through the remainder of the night, nobody slept.

Eventually, the eastern sky began to glow with the promise of the approaching day.

Without speaking, Jesus glanced at Andrew, who was manning the rudder. Jesus pointed to an area on the eastern shore of the lake. Andrew began to move the boat as the Man who calmed the storm had directed him.

Many of the disciples had spent much of their lives on the lake and knew every beach on the thirty miles of shore surrounding it. But the storm had blown them so far south that they had become disoriented. For a while, they couldn't determine exactly which shore they approached, but through the faint light they could make out a few features.

Flanked by steep, rocky bluffs, a gently sloping hill afforded them a good landing site. The disciples were looking forward to building a fire to dry their saturated gear and shivering bodies. As they neared the shore, they could see that a hillside dotted with caves rose behind it. And then the shadowy forms of tombstones emerged from the mist. They were headed toward a cemetery. Philip spoke his fear with a word that sent shivers through them all: "Gadara!"

Encounter With a Lunatic

The region of Gadara, also known as Decapolis, was established after Alexander the Great conquered the Jews. Shrines to Greco-Roman gods filled the surrounding cities, and Greeks and other Gentiles, some of them pig farmers, comprised most of the population. Revolted by both the idolatry and the unclean beasts, the Jews avoided this pagan lake district whenever possible.

However, another reason for apprehension kept the Jews at bay: chilling stories of wild men, half beast and half devil, who roamed the shores. So, as they approached the dismal scene of ancient tombs and paganism, the disciples wondered why Jesus was directing them there. Yet they dared not question the Man who could still a storm.

Like a benediction of peace, the light of the rising sun began to illuminate the shore, and the Savior and His companions landed. As Andrew secured the boat, the other disciples followed Jesus up the beach to begin collecting pieces of driftwood for a fire.

Shortly, Nathanael paused from his task and looked about, his nose tilted to the wind. Grimacing, he asked, "What is that smell?"

Thomas quipped, "Do you think it might have something to do with that herd of swine up on the hills?"

But Nathanael knew better. "No. I've smelled pigs before. This is different."

Just then, a terrifying shriek rang in the disciples' ears. As they turned toward the horrifying noise that emanated from the cemetery, a sight that frightened them more than the fury of the tempest greeted their eyes. From some dark hiding place among the tombs, a naked madman—perhaps more wild beast than human—charged toward them as if intent upon tearing them to pieces.

The petrified disciples, with nerves already worn thin by the terrifying experience of the storm, instinctively dropped their firewood and fled to their boat. Thrusting it back into the sea, they dived into it and began rowing furiously, splashing water in every direction. When they had put some distance between themselves and the shore, Andrew took inventory and noticed that Jesus was not with them. He had remained on shore.

In their haste, the disciples had deserted their Master. But the One who had stilled the tempest, who had met and conquered Satan in the wilderness, had not fled before the furious madman.

The disciples knew they had never seen a more hideous creature. Remnants of shattered chains shackled to his wrists and ankles shook violently. His bruised and bloodied flesh was torn—shredded by cuts he had deliberately made with razor-sharp stones. His eyes glared through strings of long, greasy hair caked with twigs and dirt, and his snarling mouth foamed.

Is there any humanity left in this man? the disciples wondered from their safe distance. *Or have the hordes of demons that now possess him completely blotted it out?*

As the deranged soul, gnashing his teeth, charged their Lord, He raised His hand toward the wild man in the same way He had gestured to the sea. And as if an invisible wall rose between them, the demoniac could come no nearer. Though raging with fury, he stood helpless before the Master.

Still, as contorted as was the face of this seemingly hopeless madman, Jesus could see a glimmer of pleading in his eyes.

Before Jesus had even stepped onto the sandy beach, the terrified devils knew of His approach. They dreaded the likelihood that they would soon be evicted from their captured host. And despite all the hatred and fear these demonic personalities contained, somewhere deep down inside their victim the spark of a soul still faintly glowed.

With whatever fragments were left of this man's reasoning powers he had overheard the desperate conversation of the cruel demons in his head. He learned from them who Jesus was, and that surely Jesus was his last and only hope for deliverance. As the demons roared, he threw himself down at the Savior's feet.

The worship posture of this unfortunate soul who wanted to cry out for deliverance humbled the demons within. Even so, they interrupted him with a loud shriek: "What have I to do with You, Jesus, Son of the Most High God? I implore You by God that You do not torment me" (Mark 5:7).

Jesus, ever eager to save the wretched, saw beyond the demons' attempt to stifle their host. He glimpsed the yearning soul begging for deliverance. And in a majestic voice whose tones of divine authority could be heard across the water, Jesus commanded, "Come out of the man, unclean spirit!"

Just as the storm had responded immediately to Jesus, so the poor man's body began to writhe and twist violently, as though a dozen alley cats were fighting in a burlap bag. The long series of spasms and convulsions showed that the furious demons were not going to release their victim without a struggle.

Jesus then did something that He had never done before nor would ever do again. Suspecting that Lucifer himself was orchestrating this battle, Jesus asked the demons a question: "What is your name?" Of course, He who numbers the hairs of our head and calls all the countless stars by individual names knows even the name of every fallen angel.

A wailing sound, one that human vocal chords could never produce, escaped from the man's throat. Amplified as a thousand spirits shouted in unison, resounding as if emanating from deep within some great cavernous abyss, it chilled the blood of the disciples, still cowering in the boat. The demonic cry? "My name is Legion; for we are many!"

Possessed Pigs

The demons, now resigned to their fate, knew Jesus was about to evict them from the body and mind of their victim. They knew the authority of Jesus' word is supreme. But in a pathetic lust for self-preservation, they hoped to convince Jesus not to cast them into abysmal nothingness. In a loud, unified wail, they entreated, "Please do not cast us into the deep. Let us enter the pigs."

Just up the shore from the cemetery, a large herd of two thousand pigs foraged along the hillside, grunting and wallowing in the meadow's muck. Their keepers, painfully aware of the madman's threatening habits, always tried to track his location and maintain a safe distance. Today they were huddled together, straining their eyes to see what was transpiring with their nemesis down by the lake.

Glancing first at the pigs and then back at the man before Him, Jesus said just one forceful word to the possessors: "Go!" With that, the wretched man gave one final, mighty convulsion—as if vomiting a cyclone from his belly—and then fell in a heap at the feet of his Rescuer.

Then the horde of demons that had ravaged the man fell like hail onto the mass of pigs. Instantaneously, the entire herd was awash in panic and pain. Squealing and shrieking with a deafening roar, they began to stampede toward the steep cliffs rising above the lake. The horrified keepers, huddled behind a tree for protection, could do nothing but watch as the suicidal avalanche of scavengers plunged over the cliffs, tumbled down the sharp rocks, and splashed into the water.

Then all was quiet and still, save for the stunned keepers. They crept cautiously to the bluff's edge to peer in disbelief at the churning, crimson water below. They watched as the last few pigs twitched and then disappeared beneath the surface. Not even one survived.

The keepers returned their gaze to the man they had feared—and to the One who had stood unwavering before him. They watched as Jesus led the now calm soul to the water's edge and cleansed him. They saw that the shackles and chains that had once encumbered him were now, mysteriously, broken open and strewn on the beach.

Only when they saw Jesus take off His outer robe and place it over the naked man's shoulders did they finally understand that the demons had gone from him—destroyed in their herd. Terrified and amazed, they fled to the surrounding towns and cities to recount the supernatural event they had witnessed.

Before the morning was spent, nearly every person in the region gathered on the small beach to see firsthand the transformed man and his Benefactor. Still, an unexplainable fear kept them from venturing too close, so they gazed in amazement from afar at their visitors.

The disciples, having now brought the boat back to shore, sat with Jesus and earnestly spoke to the former demoniac, still robed with Jesus' clothing. The man, who sat near his Savior's feet, had a new glint of awareness and intelligence in his eyes, from which tears of gratitude fell, leaving joyful streaks on his cheeks.

For more than an hour, the thousands of gawking spectators gaped at the small contingent gathered around the little fishing boat. The disciples, always wary, were unsettled by the menacing looks from some of the people in the crowd. They watched as a discussion between what appeared to be several prominent leaders from the surrounding communities grew increasingly animated. Though they could grasp only a few of the words being exchanged, because these people spoke Greek, they soon made out that the politicians were more upset than grateful. To them, the economic catastrophe brought about by the death of two thousand pigs outweighed the redemption of the man who had terrified them all for so long.

With disbelief they watched as the small contingent of leaders awkwardly approached Jesus and, in broken Aramaic, made their simple request: "Please leave our territory." The eyes of the disciples flared with indignation—such rudeness in this ungrateful request! For years this crazed lunatic had harassed and haunted the entire region. Now they were unharmed only because Jesus had acted. But instead of thanking Jesus or inviting Him to a banquet to honor Him for His miraculous deed, these Gentiles insulted Him!

The hurt on Jesus' face was all that expressed His disappointment—He offered no argument and launched no rebuke toward them. Jesus, knowing human hearts, simply stood up, dusted off His sandals, and motioned to the disciples that they should prepare to launch the boat.

Then the man whom Jesus had liberated, the man He had freed from the devilish horde, dived to the feet of the Savior and clutched His ankles. He pled, "Lord, let me go with you!"

With understanding love and tenderness, Jesus answered warmly, "Return to your own house, and tell what great things God has done for you."

As the disciples rowed out into open water, this man—the free man of Decapolis—stood on the shore, gazing at his Redeemer until the vessel had disappeared over the distant horizon.

Panorama of Salvation

Friend, the incredible story you have been reading is my retelling of arguably the most dramatic and profound example in Scripture of total deliverance. This story is the catalyst for everything else you will explore in this book.

In several ways, the story of Jesus' encounter with the demoniac stands apart from every other story in the New Testament. It is essentially a microcosm of the entire blueprint of redemption, illustrating the devil's ultimate, cruel designs for humanity contrasted with God's loving plan for our future.

It demonstrates in a disturbing way the reality of evil forces working to destroy our lives. But it also shows how the Lord can deliver us regardless of how hopeless our situation might appear. Indeed, it is a wonderful demonstration of God's power to cleanse and forgive any man or woman who has sunk to the murkiest depths of sin. And ultimately, it represents how the Lord can save an entire world.

In the following pages, we will mine together the deeper lessons found in this fantastic story, and we'll glean a few nuggets—some perhaps obvious, others below the surface.

I have divided this book into three sections: "Perfectly Lost," "The Deceptive Devil," and "The Divine Deliverance." These sections present the problem, the cause, and the answer. We will consider each fully before moving on to the next.

Like the story of the demoniac, the Bible's central message revolves around salvation from sin. It employs three primary characters to tell its story: the Savior, Satan, and lost souls—or Jesus, the devil, and us human beings. If you have a Bible available, I think you will find it handy to keep it within reach as you read this book.

I have combined the accounts of the demoniac's story that appear in the Gospels of Matthew, Mark, and Luke. By overlapping the various versions, we can see the whole picture in one pass. This complete picture of the story will be the springboard for the rest of our safari into the science of salvation. I encourage you to read it very carefully because, as you will see, every detail adds a new dimension to understanding God and His wonderful plan of salvation.

They came to the other side of the sea, to the country of the Gadarenes. And when He had come out of the boat, immediately there met Him out of the tombs a man with an unclean spirit, who had demons for a long time . . . exceedingly fierce, so that no one could pass that way. And he wore no clothes, nor did he live in a house but in the tombs.

And no one could bind him, not even with chains, for it had often seized him, and he was kept under guard, bound with chains and shackles; and the chains had been pulled apart and broken in pieces by him; neither could anyone tame him. And he was driven by the devil into the wilderness. And always, night and day, he was in the mountains and in the tombs, crying out and cutting himself with stones.

When he saw Jesus from afar, he ran and worshiped Him. And he cried out with a loud voice and said, "What have I to do with You, Jesus, Son of the Most High God? I implore You by God that You do not torment me before the time." For He said to him, "Come out of the man, unclean spirit!"

Then Jesus asked him, "What is your name?"

And he answered, saying, "My name is Legion; for we are many." Also he begged Him earnestly that He would not command them to go out into the abyss.

Now a large herd of many swine was feeding there near the mountains. So all the demons begged Him, saying, "Send us to the swine, that we may enter them." And at once Jesus gave them permission; He said to them, "Go."

Then the unclean spirits went out and entered the swine (there were about two thousand); and the herd ran violently down the steep place into the sea, and drowned in the sea. So those who fed the swine fled, and they told it in the city and in the country and told everything, including what had happened to the demon-possessed man. And they went out to see what it was that had happened.

Then they came to Jesus, and saw the one who had been demon-possessed and had the legion, sitting at the feet of Jesus, clothed and in his right mind. And they were afraid. And those who saw it told them how it happened to him who had been demon-possessed, and about the swine. Then they began to plead with Him to depart from their region.

And when He got into the boat, he who had been demon-possessed begged Him that he might be with Him. However, Jesus did not permit him, but said to him, "Go home to your friends, and tell them what great things the Lord has done for you, and how He has had compassion on you." And he departed and began to proclaim in Decapolis all that Jesus had done for him; and all marveled. So it was, when Jesus returned, that the multitude welcomed Him, for they were all waiting for Him.*

---

*Taken from Mark 5:1-20; Luke 8:26-40; and Matthew 8:28-34, NKJV. Please note that the Gospels of Luke and Mark tell this story about one demoniac, while Matthew recounts two demon-possessed men. The apparent discrepancy likely comes from the fact that Mark and Luke saw the second demoniac as passive and thus irrelevant to the story. For simplicity and to avoid confusion, this book will use Mark's and Luke's accounts as its foundation.

Perfectly Lost

"We know that the whole creation groaneth and travaileth in pain together until now."
—Romans 8:22, KJV

A Planet Possessed

Take a deep breath. We're going to get one more penetrating and unsettling look at the demoniac's deplorable situation before Jesus delivered him, because he's the perfect picture of total spiritual bankruptcy:

> The possessed man moves among decomposing carcasses in the shadow of the surrounding hills, snorting the cries of the foul swine. His ripped and raw flesh drags remnants of mangled shackles and chains. Screaming and moaning, his snarling mouth foaming with saliva, he wanders aimlessly among the silhouettes of caves and tombs, his stinking, naked

body followed by a cloud of flies. He continually stabs at his scarred limbs with flinty rocks, and his wild eyes glare menacingly from under his dirty, matted hair.

You're probably thinking, "OK, Doug! Enough!"

I realize this is a loathsome picture, but every component of the story, no matter how sickening, is very important. Each one tells us many crucial things about just how awful the condition of sin can be, and thus how amazing the wonderful plan of salvation really is.

Have you ever wondered about the contrast unfallen angels must see when they leave the pure, sinless glories of heaven to come to our dark, possessed planet? For them, this nameless, crazed man must represent exhibit "A" of what it means to be lost.

This fallen, possessed child of Adam living in a cemetery, surrounded by swine, also represents our fallen, unclean world under the curse of death and enslaved by the devil and his legions of minions. Our planet is now the staging ground from which Satan continues his slanderous campaign against the Creator and His government—so much so that Jesus even calls Satan "the prince of this world" (John 14:30, KJV).

Every aspect of this man's desperate condition that Scripture presents can help you and me to appreciate more fully how heaven sees the lost. Before we can understand this better and experience the

healing God offers us, we must recognize and diag-
nose the symptoms.

"Who had his dwelling among the tombs . . ."
—Mark 5:3

Dwelling With the Dead

I remember well the visit I made to the strangest
cemetery on earth while exploring the northern parts
of Cairo, Egypt. This cemetery is called the "City of
the Dead." The place hardly seems like a cemetery
because it is teeming with life and activity.

Over a span of centuries, the great Egyptian rulers of ages past built acres and acres of huge and
elaborate mausoleums and tombs. As tradition dic-
tated, each of these burial places had its own "party
room." Around the fourteenth century, thousands
of poor people seeking shelter began squatting in
these tombs. Now, this area, classified as a suburb
of Cairo, has its own ZIP code, post office, police
station, shops, electricity, running water, and sew-
erage system.

Peering into the tombs, I could see how these
people conduct their everyday lives—sleeping, cook-
ing, and eating. I was impressed with how they've
made use of the smaller gravestones, turning them
as needed into washing lines and tables. And all
through this area are stone coffins filled with human
remains—right in the middle of the current inhabitants' living space.

Archaeologists say that some of the tombs around Gadara, where our story takes place, were cut out of the steep mountainside, creating deep caves. The demoniac might have used one of these cavernous tombs for shelter after he had been driven out of town due to his deranged mind. And just as the unsaved live in constant fear of death, this poor man was daily surrounded with reminders of his bleak future.

The Bible teaches that there are only two classes of people in the world: the living and the dead. You might think this is an obvious statement, but according to God's Word, not all of the living are alive and not all of the dead are really dead.

Let me explain. Those living lives without Christ are spiritually dead. Jesus said, " 'He who has the Son has life; he who does not have the Son of God does not have life' " (1 John 5:12). On another occasion, He said, " 'Let the dead bury their own dead, but you go and preach the kingdom of God' " (Luke 9:60).

Practically speaking, this means that all those who have not had their sins forgiven are living under the death penalty. Yet when they accept Christ's forgiveness, they pass from death to life. "You He made alive, who were dead in trespasses and sins" (Ephesians 2:1).

Conversely, when a Christian dies, he or she doesn't really die—at least not the eternal death. When Lazarus perished, Jesus explained, " 'Our friend Lazarus sleeps, but I go that I may wake him up' " (John 11:11). Jesus also proclaimed, " 'Have you not read what was spoken to you by God, saying, "I am the God of Abraham, the God of Isaac, and the God of Jacob"? God is not the God of the dead, but of the living' " (Matthew 22:31, 32). Acts 7:60 affirms this truth, saying that when Stephen was murdered by stoning, "he fell asleep." Those who die in a saved condition, in Christ, are not eternally dead; they are simply resting until the resurrection.

Comfortable With a Corpse

I once read about a lady who died. That happens every day, of course; but in this case, two months passed before anyone knew about it. Her neighbors started noticing that her porch was full of mail and newspapers, and they realized that they hadn't seen her in a while. They summoned the police, who broke down the door and found her dead. They found her husband in her bedroom. He was dead too—and the medical examiner estimated that he'd been dead for at least four years! His body was virtually mummified because his wife had kept the heat turned up to about ninety degrees. She had never reported his demise—evidently, she was willing to live with the corpse so that she could continue collecting his Social Security checks!

The Bible tells us about the battle that rages between the spirit and the flesh. Millions of people want to serve God, but their carnal natures—the lust of the flesh and the pride of life—seem to chain them to their toxic lives. It's like living with a dead person. In fact, in Romans 7:24, Paul asks a penetrating question that uses this image in echoing the pleading of our hearts: "O wretched man that I am! Who will deliver me from this body of death?"

It is very probable that the apostle was referring to a frightening ancient Roman practice reserved for the most wicked criminals. Commentator Adam Clark writes, "After being scourged, the wounded prisoner would be chained to a dead body and obliged to carry it about till the contagion from the putrid mass took away his life!" An old English poem describes it this way:

> What tongue can such barbarities record,
>   Or count the slaughters of his ruthless sword?
> 'Twas not enough the good, the guiltless bled,
>   Still worse, he bound the living to the dead:
> These, limb to limb, and face to face, he joined;
>   O! monstrous crime, of unexampled kind!
> Till choked with stench, the lingering wretches lay,
>   And, in the loathed embraces, died away!
>   —Pitt

With that disturbing picture in mind, can you imagine the relief and freedom the condemned one might experience if the corpse that he'd been dragging around for days were cut away? Well, this is what the Lord does for us when we come to him with our weak, burdensome, carnal natures.

For the law of the Spirit of life in Christ Jesus has made me free from the law of sin and death . . . that the righteous requirement of the law might be fulfilled in us who do not walk according to the flesh but according to the Spirit. . . . For to be carnally minded is death, but to be spiritually minded is life and peace (Romans 8:2, 4, 6).

Dumpster Diving

You might be wondering how anyone could become comfortable with living surrounded by dead bodies. How could the demoniac live among the dead, like the people who inhabit the City of the Dead and the lady who lived for four years alongside the corpse of her husband? It might be hard to imagine, but I know it's possible, because I've experienced becoming comfortable around some very disturbing things.

For instance, when I was sixteen years old, I lived on the streets in Southern California for a few months. During that time, I had some friends who "shopped" for food in supermarket dumpsters with the same delight that other people have exploring a buffet. We called it "dumpster diving."

Having been raised in a clean, middle-class home, I was at first revolted by the disgusting habit these street friends had of fishing around for food in stinking, grocery-store garbage containers. But the longer I hung around them, the less offensive dumpster diving became. Gradually, I drew closer to the dumpster—of course, only in an advisory role! While holding my nose, I would point out dented cans or day-old bread still in its wrapper. Eventually, I began to reach over the edge to inspect ripe bananas. And then—you guessed it!—before long I was crawling into the dumpster and rooting around for "treasure." I had become intimately comfortable with garbage.

This same degrading dynamic also erodes the spiritual health of many souls. The devil knows that through constant exposure to sin—through things like morally questionable movies, magazines, and music—he can soften our convictions regarding the deadly evil of sin. It might have taken months for the lady to become comfortable with her dead husband, but the checks that kept coming made it palatable. If we tolerate sin despite finding it offensive, we'll eventually endure it until we fully embrace it.

In order for us to repent genuinely, we must recognize and appreciate the evil of sin. "Sin, that it might appear sin, was producing death in me through what is good, so that sin through the commandment might become exceedingly sinful" (Romans 7:13).

"He wore no clothes."—Luke 8:27

The Naked Truth

Most of us never feel much gratitude for our clothing, but some people actually owe their lives to what they wear! For instance, to survive in the extreme temperatures and vacuum of space, astronauts need special spacesuits. These thick outfits supply oxygen, maintain pressure, keep body temperature controlled, and monitor blood pressure and heart rhythm.

When Neil Armstrong sealed his place in history as the first man to walk on the moon during the Apollo 11 mission, his suit was specially designed to provide a life-sustaining environment during periods of extravehicular activity and unpressurized spacecraft operations. The custom-fitted suit permitted maximum mobility and could be worn with relative comfort for up to 115 hours outside the spacecraft or for fourteen days in an unpressurized mode.

Astronauts must put an enormous amount of trust in their spacesuits. One described the eerie feeling he got when he realized that while outside the space capsule, just one-quarter inch of material lay between him and eternity. Now that's important clothing!

Back in Gadara, however, the frost of the winter mornings made the demoniac's naked frame shiver. And through the scorching summer, his leathery skin would burn. But neither heat nor cold nor even shame would lead him to cover his naked limbs.

When it comes to clothing, human beings differ from every other creature. All the other creatures in God's kingdom are "born with their clothes on," so to speak. The covering they need grows from the inside out. Some animals even shed their old clothes periodically and develop new ones. Human beings are the only creatures whose clothes must come from the outside.

The Bible tells us that Adam and Eve first wore artificial clothing after they ate the forbidden fruit in the Garden of Eden. Genesis 3:7 (KJV) says, "The eyes of them both were opened, and they knew that they were naked; and they sewed fig leaves together, and made themselves aprons."

Our first parents had the sense and modesty to recognize when they were naked and to seek a remedy. Not everybody feels that natural yearning to be covered.

When I was about seventeen, I lived as a hermit in a mountain cave above Palm Springs. During that time, I never wore clothes while in the vicinity of my "home." At first I was painfully aware that something was missing, but after going naked for several weeks, I rarely thought about it. Like dumpster diving, you can get used to almost anything if you do it long enough.

Once or twice a week, I would hike down to the city to panhandle for money in front of the local supermarket. I always carried my clothes in a little bundle at the bottom of my backpack. When I approached the outskirts of civilization, I would stop and dress before venturing into the city limits.

On one occasion, I felt particularly enthusiastic about going to town because I had some money and an exciting list of small things to purchase. When I reached the top of the ridge, I felt exhilarated! It was a spring morning in the desert, the sun was just rising, and everything was glowing with a brazen, beautiful color—all the hills, the cactus, and even my skin looked golden.

Playing my flute, I bebopped down the mountain and walked right past the big rock where I usually stopped to put on my clothes. Still enthralled, I didn't notice that I was venturing into the city limits wearing nothing but a backpack, some hiking boots, and a friendly smile.

As I came around a bend in the trail screened by a large bush, I saw a nicely dressed family—a father, a mother, and two daughters—taking a Sunday stroll and enjoying the desert flowers. I felt so good that I even offered them a wave and a grin.

They all froze!

As shock ripped through the family, the mother closed her eyes and hid her face against the father's chest, the two little girls each grabbed one of their father's legs and turned away, and even the father closed his eyes!

I instinctively assumed that some terrifyingly hideous monster was looming behind me, and I snapped around. But I didn't see anything. I wondered, *What did they see that made them react with such horror?* Then it dawned on me. They were looking at me—and I was naked! Overwhelmed with shame, I slipped behind the closest bush and quickly dressed.

What had happened to me? I felt perfectly fine the moment before I saw this family. They hadn't touched me, and they said nothing to me. Yet after that encounter, I felt awful. What made the difference? I saw myself through their eyes, and I saw that I was naked.

All of us would be much healthier if we would get a fresh look at ourselves through God's eyes. We might discover that we're naked too! The Bible says that one of the most serious problems His own people face in the last days is that they are naked. Actually, the problem is not just that they're naked, but that they're naked and don't know it. God says, "[You] do not know that you are wretched, miserable, poor, blind, and naked" (Revelation 3:17).

A Natural Sense of Shame

An Old Testament prophet wrote, "The unjust knows no shame" (Zephaniah 3:5).

We're living in a society very aware of psychology. Everywhere we turn, people are being told, "Don't feel bad!" Popular opinion says, "Guilt is bad—it's destructive." Of course, there's some truth to that, but we ought to feel guilty when we are guilty. We shouldn't feel good about doing bad.

The Lord wants us to feel guilt and conviction long enough and hard enough for it to motivate us to come to Him for forgiveness. He doesn't want us to remain in a state of perpetual mourning, but we must become aware of our fallen condition before He can cleanse and restore us. And how can we ever be sorry for our sins if we don't recognize our wretched state?

Once we do see our lowly state and fall to our knees for forgiveness, God can activate His power in our lives. "Humble yourselves in the sight of the Lord, and He will lift you up" (James 4:10).

When Adam and Eve disobeyed God, the light that clothed them was extinguished. They were suddenly aware of their nakedness and felt a natural sense of shame (see Genesis 3:10). As we do when we sin, the first pair tried to cover themselves to hide their guilt—in their case with fig leaves. But they soon realized that the leaves wouldn't last.

After the couple acknowledged their guilt to God, He gave them coats of skins.

Did you catch that? *Skins!* Something had to die to cover their naked bodies, just as Jesus had to die to cover our sins.

When the prodigal son returned home, acknowledging his failures, his father received him, embraced him, kissed him, and then covered his filth and nakedness with his own "best" robe. Likewise, Jesus is waiting to clothe us with His righteousness, but we must first come home as we are.

After Jesus delivered the demoniac, we find that man sitting at Jesus' feet, clothed, and in his right mind (see Luke 8:35). Author Malcolm Muggeridge said, "Psychiatrists require many sessions to relieve a patient from feelings of guilt which have made him sick in body and mind; Jesus' power of spiritual and moral persuasion was so overwhelming that he could produce the same effect just by saying: 'Thy sins be forgiven thee.' "

He "fled from them naked."—Mark 14:52

Naked Retreat

Each year the city of Pamplona, Spain, hosts the traditional "running of the bulls." Many brave souls tempt fate at this dangerous festival, which results in many injuries and even some fatalities. Six bulls and six steers chase some two thousand people through the narrow, cobblestone streets.

One year a news program broadcast video footage from the event of one bold fool who, in an apparent display of machismo bravado, ran directly toward a bull in an arena to taunt it. He soon found himself, quite literally, on the horns of a dilemma. The bull managed to hook the man's pants and shook him as if he was nothing but a rag doll—until the fellow lost his pants and underwear! The closing shot showed the man fleeing away naked, no doubt ashamed, as the spectators roared with laughter. It is generally true that when we toy with Satan, we end up fleeing, naked and ashamed.

The Bible shares a very interesting story in connection with the betrayal and arrest of Jesus. As a mob carried Him away, an unnamed man attempted to follow, to observe Jesus' fate: "A certain young man followed Him, having a linen cloth thrown around his naked body. And the young men laid hold of him, and he left the linen cloth and fled from them naked" (Mark 14:51, 52). Many scholars believe this was Mark himself.

BROKEN CHAINS

This depicts the nature of Satan and sin, a deadly duo who will strip you and send you running in shame. After Adam and Eve ate the forbidden fruit and their luminous robes faded, they felt shame because of their nakedness. When God came looking for them, He found them trembling in the bushes (see Genesis 3:7, 8).

A common practice in many ancient cultures was to strip captives taken in war and march them along the streets naked (see 2 Chronicles 28:15). In the same way, Satan wants to flaunt and humiliate his prisoners by stripping them of their dignity and parading their shame before heaven.

The book of Acts tells of some young men who recklessly attempted to exorcise an evil spirit from a possessed person. Their attempt resulted in yet another naked retreat. "The man in whom the evil spirit was leaped on them, overpowered them, and prevailed against them, so that they fled out of that house naked and wounded" (Acts 19:16). The Bible records other instances that fit this pattern in which the devil disrobes the disobedient. For instance, Noah got drunk and then stumbled around naked (see Genesis 9:21), and when the children of Israel worshiped the golden calf, they were naked (see Exodus 32:25, KJV).

"Nor did he live in a house but in the tombs."
—*Luke 8:27*

Sin Separates

Even emotionally healthy people are prone to become eccentric when they don't have the social interaction with others that helps to keep our thoughts balanced. The menacing evil spirits that possessed the demoniac plunged him into false perceptions of reality and frequently left him muttering incoherently—thus isolating him, like a leper, from family, friends, and normal society. This only compounded his problems.

A simple and dependable law in life is that love unites and sin separates. Isaiah wrote, "Your iniquities have separated between you and your God" (Isaiah 59:2, KJV). Sin separates us from God. Just as light and darkness cannot coexist, sin automatically drives us from God.

Sin separates us from one another. The epidemic of divorce in our culture provides us with plenty evidence for this. "Because iniquity shall abound, the love of many shall wax cold" (Matthew 24:12, KJV).

And ultimately, sin causes divisions within our own selves. The medicated masses, burdened by guilt springing largely from a low self-esteem, are evidence of this.

Jesus came to end all this separation. His love is the ladder, the link, that bridges heaven and earth. It is His love that brings reconciliation to relationships broken by sin. "In Christ Jesus you who once were far off have been made near by the blood of Christ. For He Himself is our peace, who has made both one, and has broken down the middle wall of division between us" (Ephesians 2:13, 14).

∞

He was "bound with chains and shackles."
—Luke 8:29

Adorned With Chains

In the Middle Ages, a blacksmith was imprisoned for a serious crime and was chained to prevent any attempt at escape. The blacksmith had made many chains himself, so he began to examine with anxious interest the one that bound him. His experience taught him that the chains other blacksmiths made often were flawed, and he hoped to discover a flaw in the one that bound him. But suddenly his hope faded. Marks on the chain revealed that he had made it—and he had worked hard to earn the reputation of making flawless, unbreakable chains. He had no hope of ever breaking free.

The shattered chains that adorned the hands and feet of the demoniac represent the sins that bind each sinner and his or her ability to resist.* Like the blacksmith, most of us are bound with

---

*These chains also represent the approaching judgment that will cause Satan, his angels, and all who follow him to tremble. "The angels who did not keep their proper domain, but left their own habitation, He has reserved in everlasting chains under darkness for the judgment of the great day" (Jude 6; see also 2 Peter 2:4).

chains of our own forging. "His own iniquities entrap the wicked man, and he is caught in the cords of his sin" (Proverbs 5:22). Samuel Johnson echoed this proverb when he said, "The chains of a bad habit are too weak to be felt until they are too strong to be broken."*

I have a radical theory. I think that God created all humans to be addicts. That's right—each of us is an addict, and God designed us that way! That is, the Creator made us to be addicted to Him. So, when people reject Him, they struggle in vain to fill that cavernous black hole with some other obsession. As a result, people become subject to a broad spectrum of addictions. Some become workaholics. Some become addicted to food, and suffer bulimia, anorexia, or obesity. Some choose alcohol, drugs, or cigarettes. For others, it's sex, or music. For still others, it's fashion and outward appearance; they consume themselves with materialism and vanity. There are also those who become addicted to other people in twisted, co-dependent relationships.

All these addictions are misguided attempts to fill a void designed for God. But it's only in God's love that we will find true joy, peace, and satisfaction.

---

*I imagine that the ten cities of Decapolis might have had an ongoing contest to see who could capture and control the local madman. Those ten cities might be seen as a type of the Ten Commandments that the demoniac refused to keep. These commandments work like chains and fetters to restrain sinners from their wicked course. Like the demoniac, though, sinners stubbornly break those bands asunder.

BROKEN CHAINS

A story in the Bible offers us a great illustration of encouragement. The apostle Peter was hopelessly imprisoned, held by two chains and bound for judgment. But when he obeyed the simple instructions of an angel, the chains miraculously fell from his hands. The Bible records it like this:

The night before Peter was to be placed on trial, he was asleep, chained between two soldiers, with others standing guard at the prison gate. Suddenly, there was a bright light in the cell, and an angel of the Lord stood before Peter. The angel tapped him on the side to awaken him and said, "Quick! Get up!" And the chains fell off his wrists (Acts 12:6, 7, NLT).

The beauty here is that God pursues us, meeting us where we are—with whatever chains bind us. As Jesus came to the demoniac's cemetery and the angel came to Peter's death-row cell, so the Spirit comes to us, held captive as we are by Satan. "The people who walked in darkness have seen a great light; those who dwelt in the land of the shadow of death, upon them a light has shined" (Isaiah 9:2).

We see this gospel message when Peter was cleaning his dirty nets, when Matthew was counting his dirty money, and when Mary Magdalene was in the temple after being caught in a dirty act. Jesus meets us in our prison as He met Peter, Matthew, and Mary, and He invites us to leave our chains behind and follow Him—not by compulsion but as willing servants.

On July 31, 1838, a large company of slaves gathered on a beach in Jamaica for a solemn yet joyous occasion. Slavery was to be abolished the next day. These slaves had constructed a large mahogany coffin and placed it next to a deep grave that they had dug. That evening, they placed symbols of their enslavement in the coffin—chains, leg-irons, whips, and padlocks. A few minutes before midnight, they lowered the box into the grave. Then, as these slaves pushed sand into the hole, they joined their voices to sing the doxology: "Praise God from whom all blessings flow." Now they were free. The next day, many of these returned to work in the fields or on the docks—but this time as free men and women.

Similarly, people who accept Christ's death are freed from their slavery to sin. And like those former slaves, when they're in heaven, they'll be free from the very reminder and presence of sin. "God be thanked that though you were slaves of sin, yet you obeyed from the heart that form of doctrine to which you were delivered. And having been set free from sin, you became slaves of righteousness" (Romans 6:17, 18).

He was "exceeding fierce, so that no man might pass by that way."—Matthew 8:28

Raging Hearts

The term *road rage* has been added to our vocabulary quite recently. It names an alarming phenomenon in North America. Angry motorists shoot and kill—or deliberately chase down and crash their cars into—other drivers whom they believe have executed some inconsiderate or otherwise offensive maneuver. This growing practice has become so much of a problem that the Automobile Association of America ran a series of television ads to teach drivers both how to keep their cool and how to avoid becoming victims.

Matthew tells us that the demoniac was furious and raging, attacking anyone who ventured to take the road past the tombs he inhabited. He was more like an animal than a human being. Likewise, I believe that when people lose their temper, they can be—at least temporarily—demon possessed.

The following story will help illustrate my reasons for this conviction: A young mother began watching some *Amazing Facts* TV programs and felt drawn to commit her life to Jesus. She began studying the Bible and believing the truth it contains. She told her live-in boyfriend that they must either marry or separate.

This ultimatum infuriated the boyfriend. One evening, as the woman was nailing a copy of the Ten Commandments to the wall, he grabbed the hammer out of her hand and began bludgeoning her with it. The commotion caused their baby in the adjoining room to begin crying. The man, thinking he had killed his girlfriend, went into the next room and killed the child. The couple's landlord heard the noise and stormed in to see what was happening. When the enraged boyfriend charged him, the landlord shot and killed him.

I learned of the terrible tragedy when the devastated young woman—who, miraculously, had survived with only minor injuries—contacted me. She called to ask if I would conduct the funeral for her baby, the boy whose father had murdered him because he lost his temper.

It was the fact that the father's outburst happened when the mother posted the Ten Commandments on the wall that struck me most. I thought it to be significant evidence of the satanic inspiration of the whole incident. The devil especially hates the law of God because that law identifies sin. Scripture tells us that sin is the transgression of the law (see 1 John 3:4, KJV).

We are truly living in the "age of rage." People are simmering and seething inside. Ulcers and antacids are not the only byproducts of an angry world—every day, headlines are peppered with stories of people losing their tempers and committing some horrific act of violence against total strangers, fellow workers, or—even more commonly—members of their own families.*

We need to take note of this trend. Bible prophecy has warned us that in the last days, unbridled anger, tirades, and temper tantrums would become the

---

*It's perhaps little coincidence that the first act of murder recorded in the Bible happened when a man lost his temper and killed his brother (see Genesis 4:3-8).

norm. The apostle Paul said that anger is one of the fruits of the flesh. "The works of the flesh are evident, which are: adultery, fornication, uncleanness, lewdness, idolatry, sorcery, hatred, contentions, jealousies, outbursts of wrath" (Galatians 5:19, 20).

Anger Is Very Costly

An Italian proverb warns, "Anger is a very expensive commodity." The great maestro Toscanini was well known for his ferocious outbursts of anger. When members of his orchestra played badly, he would seize anything in sight and hurl it to the floor.

During one rehearsal, someone played a flat note. Toscanini reacted by grabbing his own watch, which was very valuable, and smashing it beyond repair. Shortly after, he received from his devoted musicians a luxurious, velvet-lined box containing two watches—one, a beautiful gold timepiece; the other, a cheap watch on which was inscribed "For rehearsals only."

More recently, one talented athlete lost his temper and struck his coach, costing himself a thirty-two-million-dollar contract. And heavyweight boxer Mike Tyson "popped his cork" during one boxing match and proceeded to bite off a piece of his opponent's ear! That outburst cost him millions. The last I heard, Tyson had squandered more than three hundred million dollars in winnings and was bankrupt.

However, most people don't lose that kind of money because of their anger. So, some think a bad temper is just an inherited idiosyncrasy that shouldn't be taken too seriously. As long as their tantrums occur infrequently, there's no need to worry. "It's just part of our nature," they say. But the Bible lists wrathful outbursts as one of the works of the flesh, which means that they are devil-inspired and not something to be taken lightly. We can't pass them off jokingly by saying, "Well, that's just the way my family is," or, "I can't help it—I'm Irish!" Biblically, uncontrolled anger is a sin, and there's no excuse for sin.

While the Bible tells of no monetary losses because of anger, you'll find in it stories of some other staggering costs associated with just a momentary loss of temper. For instance, although Moses experienced forty years of miracles, God didn't permit him to lead the children of Israel into the Promised Land. Why? Because he lost his temper on the very borders of Canaan. As Will Rogers said, "Don't fly into a rage unless you're prepared for a rough landing."

Those who lose their tempers don't realize that they are at least momentarily demon-possessed. When you lose your temper, the devil is the one who finds it—and before you know it, you'll be manifesting the fruits of the flesh. Countless marriages have died because someone in a delirious rage thoughtlessly spoke cutting words that they couldn't retract. Wars have started in which multiplied millions perished because some ruler, in anger, made a rash decision.

Conversely, Jesus is known for His self-composed meekness. Those who follow Him will—and should—model His gentle patience.

Anger Destroys Us

As the myth goes, Sinbad and his sailors landed on a tropical island and saw, high up in the palm trees, coconuts that could quench their thirst and satisfy their hunger. Unable to reach the coconuts, Sinbad and his men began throwing stones and sticks at some chattering monkeys high in the trees. Enraged, the monkeys plucked the coconuts and hurled them down at the men—exactly what Sinbad wanted.

This is a good illustration of how when indulging our anger, we play into the devil's hands.

Thomas à Kempis said, "When anger enters the mind, wisdom departs." Someone else opined, "The less water in the pot, the quicker it boils." Basically, a short fuse indicates a lack of wisdom. If you are constantly giving everybody "a piece of your mind," eventually, you might not have any left—as the frustrated teacher once sputtered to her class, "You have made me so think, I can't mad straight!"*

---

[5] My dear wife, Karen, made a similar slip of the lip in church one day. I pastor a fair-sized church, and before the church service, while many of the members were visiting in the courtyard, our two youngest boys, Stephen and Nathan, became very rambunctious despite their mother's gentle and constant pleadings. Exasperated, she subconsciously scrambled their names and shouted "Satan, come here!" Of course, this produced some surprised looks among the parents standing near!

I've heard some people say, "Losing your temper is good for your health. We all need to vent from time to time to let off some steam." I don't believe that for a minute. In fact, the Bible teaches the opposite. When the king of Judah lost his temper in the house of God, he came down with leprosy. "Uzziah became furious; and he had a censer in his hand to burn incense. And while he was angry with the priests, leprosy broke out on his forehead, before the priests in the house of the LORD" (2 Chronicles 26:19).

Often, anger actually does produce visible symptoms: a red face, swollen neck veins, clenched fists, and a stumbling for words. Harvard researcher Dr. Walter Cannon describes its more insidious, invisible symptoms:

> Respiration deepens; the heart beats more rapidly; the arterial pressure rises; the blood is shifted from the stomach and intestines to the heart, central nervous system, and the muscles; the processes of the alimentary canal cease; sugar is freed from the reserves in the liver; the spleen contracts and discharges its contents of concentrated corpuscles, and adrenaline is secreted. The angry person's vision may also be blurred, because anger clouds the visual centers of the brain.

I sometimes wonder just how many people are physically ill because they are simmering or bitter inside. I know people spend millions of dollars on sedatives every year in the attempt to calm their raging hearts. The Bible says, "A merry heart does good, like medicine" (Proverbs 17:22). If that's true, it's probably safe to say that the opposite is true also—that anger, bitterness, and an unforgiving spirit can make a person sick.

Christians must learn to release all their bitter anger through Jesus. He said, "Come to Me, all you who labor and are heavy laden, and I will give you rest" (Matthew 11:28).

"Neither could any man tame him."
—Mark 5:4, KJV

Taming a Wild Heart

The flamboyant duo Siegfried and Roy had performed in the Mirage Hotel on the Las Vegas strip for nearly three decades. Hundreds of thousands of spectators had come to see their magic show, highlighted by the performance of very large and beautiful white tigers. Roy Horn spent many years training the giant cats to obey his commands. In his attempts to tame the beasts, he would go so far as to eat, swim, and sleep with them.

Then, on October 3, 2003, without explanation, a seven-year-old white tiger that had known Horn since it was a cub attacked him in front of a live audience on the magician's fifty-ninth birthday. About halfway through the show, the tiger lunged at Horn and dragged him off stage like a toy. Horn's near fatal injuries will probably prevent him from ever continuing his animal act.

The Bible teaches, "The heart is deceitful above all things, and desperately wicked; who can know it?" (Jeremiah 17:9). Our hearts are like unpredictable wild beasts; we do not and cannot know them.

The prophet Balaam thought he could resist the rewards of King Balak, but he sold out through misguided rationalization. And Samson thought he could toy with and tease the temptress Delilah. He didn't recognize the weakness in his own heart.

When Jesus was here in person, Peter, one of the disciples closest to Him, thought he knew his own heart. Jesus warned him of his betrayal beforehand, but Peter vowed, "Even if I have to die with You, I will not deny You!" (Matthew 26:35). Of course, three times on that very night, Peter denied that he knew Jesus.

We all struggle with these wild and unpredictable, Jekyll-and-Hyde swings of nature. Paul wrote, "I don't understand myself at all, for I really want to do what is right but I don't do it. Instead, I do the very thing I hate" (Romans 7:15, NLV). Human methods fail to transform our selfish, rebellious, and depraved hearts. In fact, true conversion is not heart surgery, but rather a heart transplant. God has promised, "I will give you a new heart and put a new spirit within you; I will take the heart of stone out of your flesh" (Ezekiel 36:26).

BROKEN CHAINS

We can't control our sinful nature. It's only when we allow Jesus' heart to replace our corrupted hearts that the sin-nature can be brought into subjection. Only Jesus, as our Lord and Master, can tame the "old man" within us. "Then you will find rest for your souls" (Jeremiah 6:16).

"Always, night and day, he was . . . crying."
—Mark 5:5, KJV

Always Crying

After the first day of fierce fighting in the Civil War battle of Fredericksburg, Virginia, hundreds of wounded and bleeding Union soldiers lay crying on the battlefield. Artillery fire prevented their relief all through the night and most of the second day of the conflict, so every moment the soldiers on the battle lines could hear their agonized cries, "Water! Water!"

Always restless, always wailing, like dark waves that rolled from his captive heart through his vocal cords, came the demoniac's constant mournful cries. Echoes of the continual cries of this poor, lost soul will roll throughout the universe from those unhappy souls who will be eternally separated from God's presence. "The king said to the servants, 'Bind him hand and foot, take him away, and cast him into outer darkness; there will be weeping and gnashing of teeth'" (Matthew 22:13). "'There is no peace,' says the LORD, 'for the wicked'" (Isaiah 48:22).

According to commentator Kenneth S. Wuest, the word *crying* indicates "a loud scream or shriek."* Can you imagine the awful fear that must have possessed the townspeople as the blood-curdling, animalistic screams of the demoniac echoed eerily through the mountains and awakened them in the stillness of the night?

In his book *The Valiant Papers*, Calvin Miller wrote, "Crying is common in this world. . . . Laughter can be heard here and there, but by and large, weeping predominates. With maturity the sound and reason for crying changes, but never does it stop. All infants do it everywhere—even in public. By adulthood most crying is done alone and in the dark."

Miller's thoughts find substantiation in the Bible. Paul observed, "We know that the whole creation groaneth and travaileth in pain together until now" (Romans 8:22, KJV). But let's return to the story of the Union soldiers wailing on the battlefield, as told through the pen of John W. Halliday:

> Soon a noble Southern soldier, Sergeant Richard Kirkland, rose above the love for his own life, and told General Kershaw, "I can't stand this any longer! Those poor souls have been praying and crying all night and all day, and it's more than I can bear! I ask your permission to go and give them water."

Wuest's Word Studies From the Greek New Testament, pg. 101.

"But as soon as you show yourself to the enemy," warned the general, "you will be shot at!"

"Yes, sir," the soldier answered. "But to carry a little comfort to those poor dying men, I'm willing."

The general hesitated, but his heart was also touched with his subordinate's same sympathy. "Kirkland, it's sending you to your death, but I cannot oppose such a motive as yours. I hope God will protect you. Go."

So the brave soldier, furnished with a supply of water, stepped over the stone rampart and began his work of Christ-like mercy. Wondering eyes beheld him as he knelt by the nearest sufferer, tenderly raised his head, and held the refreshing cup to his parched lips. Every soldier in the blue Union line understood the tender mission of the man in gray, and not a single shot was fired. For over an hour, one after another of the crying, wounded and dying was given refreshing drink, had his cramped or mangled limbs straightened, his head cushioned on his knapsack, and was covered with his coat or blanket as tenderly as though by his own mother.

So also is it on life's great battlefield, where souls are crying and dying from the fearful effects of sin. They are thirsty for the water of life, with none to reach out to them the refreshing draft they so crave, except the One who stepped over the ramparts of heaven and came down to risk His all on the cross of Calvary to rescue them from their sins by giving to them the water of everlasting life.

Henry Ward Beecher said, "God washes the eyes by tears until they can behold the invisible land where tears shall come no more." There, Jesus will come and wipe the tears from our eyes. "Surely he has borne our griefs, and carried our sorrows" (Isaiah 53:4).

For the lost, there is always crying within. As the demoniac, so are the unsaved. But there is very good news for the Christian: this crying is not chronic. "Weeping may endure for a night, But joy comes in the morning" (Psalm 30:5).

"Always, night and day, he was . . . cutting himself with stones."—Mark 5:5, KJV

Cutting Ourselves

Doctors say that self-mutilation is on the rise as a medical problem. It is defined as any form of compulsive self-harm to the body not intended to produce death. It is most often performed to release emotional pain, anger, or anxiety; to rebel against authority; or to feel in control. Some common forms of self-mutilation are: cutting the skin with a sharp object (the most common), burning the skin, picking at the skin, punching one's self, sticking one's self with a needle, banging the head, pressing the eyes, biting the fingers or arms, and pulling one's own hair.

Most of us would be quick to recognize that people in the practice of cutting or gouging themselves with rocks or knives have a severe mental or emotional disturbance, but these practices are no more common than are injurious forms of religious zealotry. In 1973, an overzealous Roman Catholic, Patrice Tamao, of the Dominican Republic, allowed himself to be crucified as thousands watched on television. Patrice had three 6-inch stainless-steel nails driven through his hands and feet. He intended to stay on the cross for forty-eight hours; but when an infection developed, he requested to be taken down. He'd been crucified for twenty hours. It appears that the demoniac was also trying to atone for his sins with his own blood. If Jesus hadn't delivered him, he might have eventually bled to death.

This practice of trying to gain merit with God by inflicting physical punishment on one's self lies at the foundation of many false religions. In some cases, the worshipers might flog themselves or make long pilgrimages on bloody knees. Whatever the case, any effort we make to atone for our sins by punishing ourselves amounts to nothing more than cutting ourselves with stones. Such efforts are about as effective as it would be if airline passengers were to try to help the pilots of a luxury 747 by flapping their arms as the plane flew across the ocean.

The apostle Paul wrote, "Though I give my body to be burned, but have not love, it profits me nothing" (1 Corinthians 13:3). And he reminded us that such an attitude is horribly misguided: "By grace you have been saved through faith, and that not of yourselves; it is the gift of God" (Ephesians 2:8).

In fact, any effort we make to atone for our sins by deliberately inflicting suffering on ourselves is an insult to the sacrifice and sufferings of God's Son.

Body Piercing

More than at any other time in American history, people today are mutilating their bodies in a misguided sacrifice to the god of fad and fashion. Multiple ear piercings, eyebrow and nose rings, and tongue studs all testify to the self-destructive influence the devil exerts on our culture. My heart aches for the young people of our generation, and some older ones too, who seem oblivious to the pagan and satanic history of body piercing and tattoos.*

Scripture tells us what happened when the devil-worshiping prophets of Baal tried to attract the attention of their gods by mutilating their bodies. "They cried aloud, and cut themselves, as was their cus-

---

*I have always believed that God created our bodies with the appropriate number of holes. It has never been His plan for us to add to or diminish that number.

tom, with knives and lances, until the blood gushed out on them" (1 Kings 18:28). God warns strongly that we aren't to follow this example. "You shall not make any cuttings in your flesh for the dead, nor tattoo any marks on you: I am the Lord" (Leviticus 19:28). In fact, the Bible plainly teaches that our bodies are the temple of God, and if "anyone defiles the temple of God, God will destroy him. For the temple of God is holy, which temple you are" (1 Corinthians 3: 16, 17).

Imagine a gang of vandals spraying obscene graffiti on the side of a beautiful cathedral, gouging the pure white marble walls with a jackhammer, or hurling stones through the luminous stained-glass windows. This is what the devil wants us to do to our bodies, which are to be God's holy property and dwelling place. "I beseech you therefore, brethren, by the mercies of God, that you present your bodies a living sacrifice, holy, acceptable to God, which is your reasonable service. And do not be conformed to this world, but be transformed by the renewing of your mind, that you may prove what is that good and acceptable and perfect will of God" (Romans 12:1, 2).

A rattlesnake trapped by a fire can become so frenzied that it will actually bite itself with its deadly fangs. Likewise, many who follow the devil have an inner sense of their impending doom, and they frequently lash out by hurting themselves. Satan, who knows his time is short, wants to take down with him as many as he can (Revelation 12:12). One of the ways he best serves this purpose is by leading people to destroy themselves.

Humans are just pawns in the great cosmic conflict between Christ and Satan. Ultimately, the devil's hatred for humans is an extension of his rabid hatred for Jesus. He knows how much Jesus loves the human race; he knows better than we do how much the Son of God gave up when He came to earth in the form of a man to redeem us. Remember, Satan once lived as an unfallen being in the presence of the Almighty.

Satan's preoccupation with body piercing might even come from the piercing wounds Jesus received from the thorns, nails, and a spear. Satan may not understand why Jesus loves us as He does, but he knows the depths of His love. And he recognizes that he can best grieve the Lord by hurting those He loves. He will do whatever it takes, even demon-possession, to make sure we never see Jesus' love for us. We'll talk about this more in the next section.

Trading Places

There's a story about two Filipino brothers, identical twins, who lived in Manila and made their living by driving jeepneys, Filipino taxis. Though they were twins and had similar jobs, they lived very different lives. One was married and had children; the other was single. Then one day, the married brother accidentally struck and killed a tourist with his taxi. Accused of reckless driving, the twin was sentenced to twenty years in the notorious Manila prison—a devastating fate that would leave his wife and children without an income.

One day, his twin came to visit him in prison. He said, "Brother, your family desperately needs you. Put on my clothes and take my visitor's pass, and I will put on your prison uniform and serve the rest of your sentence. Go to your family." So, while the guards were not looking, the twins exchanged clothes, and the married brother walked out of the prison unchallenged. Do you think the twin who was freed could ever stop thinking about the sacrifice that his brother made in trading places with him?

I would be remiss if I left this section dealing with the vivid symbols of sin found in the demoniac story without addressing one of the most crucial ones. The condition of the lost madman presents the ultimate picture of sin: the demoniac was poor, naked, unclean, separated from God, tormented by devils, and dwelling near death.

Did you catch that, friend? Do you see where I am going? I just described the condition of Jesus on the cross! When our Lord suffered and died for our sins, He embraced the experience of the lost.

"You know the grace of our Lord Jesus Christ, that though He was rich, yet for your sakes He became poor, that you through His poverty might become rich" (2 Corinthians 8:9). Jesus experienced the shame and nakedness of the demoniac so that His rich robes might clothe us.

"He was wounded for our transgressions, He was bruised for our iniquities; the chastisement for our peace was upon Him, and by His stripes we are healed" (Isaiah 53:5). Like the madman, Jesus was tortured and tormented by legions of evil angels. He was separated from humans and God that He might restore our relationships with our Lord and our neighbor. The demoniac's hands and feet were scarred by those who tried to confine him—as Jesus' hands and feet were wounded by those who fastened Him to the cross.

We can go further. Just as unclean pigs surrounded the demoniac, dogs surrounded Jesus. "Dogs have surrounded Me; the congregation of the wicked has enclosed Me. They pierced My hands and My feet" (Psalm 22:16). "Then some began to spit on Him" (Mark 14:65). Covered with blood and spit, Jesus became unclean.

And just as the demoniac lived by a burial ground, so Jesus was crucified near a cemetery. "Now in the place where He was crucified there was a garden, and in the garden a new tomb in which no one had yet been laid" (John 19:41).

Jesus took our weakness that we might have His strength. He was separated from God and human beings that we might be united. He took the humiliation that we deserve and offered us the glory that was His.

Christ was treated as we deserve, that we might be treated as He deserves. He was condemned for our sins, in which He had no share, that we might be justified by His righteousness, in which we had no share. He suffered the death which was ours, that we might receive the life which was His. With His stripes we are healed.*

When Jesus saved and liberated the demoniac from his wretched condition, He was in effect saying, "I will soon take your misery upon myself."

---

*Ellen G. White, *The Desire of Ages* (Nampa, Idaho: Pacific Press, 1940), 25.

The Deceptive Devil

"Woe to the inhabitants of the earth and the sea!
For the devil has come down to you, having great wrath,
because he knows that he has a short time."
—Revelation 12:12

Knowing Your Enemy

Someone has estimated that between 3600 B.C. and the present, human beings have fought in 14,531 wars. During that same period, we've had more than 5,300 years of war, compared to about 290 years of peace.

A ferocious war is raging between the forces of good and evil. It's a cosmic conflict between Christ and Satan, light and darkness, love and selfishness. And as was true of the demoniac, this war takes place in the heart and mind of every human soul. I have no doubt that you have felt this combat being waged in your own heart.

These daily skirmishes with temptation have life-or-death consequences. To fight this spiritual war, you and I need spiritual weapons. "For though we walk in the flesh, we do not war according to the flesh. For the weapons of our warfare are not carnal but mighty in God for pulling down strongholds" (2 Corinthians 10:3, 4). And we must know our enemy, the devil.

Christians must avoid two extremes when considering satanic activity. As C. S. Lewis aptly put it:

There are two equal and opposite errors into which our race can fall about the devils. One is to disbelieve in their existence. The other is to believe, and to feel an excessive and unhealthy interest in them. They themselves are equally pleased by both errors, and hail a materialist or a magician with the same delight.

With this concept of balance in mind, let's remember that one of the key components of winning a war is understanding the *modus operandi* of our enemy. The coaches and scouts of professional football teams study videotapes of opposing teams to understand their strategies better and discover ways to counteract their various plays. Similarly, before a championship fight, professional boxers analyze and evaluate every maneuver of their opponent.

I don't intend to give undue attention to the devil here; the principal message in the Bible is Jesus Christ and how we can live for the glory of God. But Scripture does record a great deal about our archenemy. Satan, the serpent, appears frequently from Genesis to Revelation. So, as Mark Twain said, "We may not pay [Satan] reverence, for that would be indiscreet; but we can at least respect his talents."

So, to understand better how the demoniac came to be possessed by these armies of darkness, it is both prudent and profitable for us to dedicate substantial time to understanding the deadly devices of the devil. While you may not enjoy this ominous section as well as you do other parts of this book, you can be sure it is the one that Satan fears most and would prefer that you neglect.

The legions of devils that possessed the nameless man in our story were not without a leader. You can be sure that Satan wasn't vacationing on the French Riviera when Jesus had this showdown with the army of demons on the beach of Gadara. And even though they are not specifically mentioned, you can be sure that the angels of God were also stationed around Jesus.

In other words, the war that began in heaven was continuing right here on earth with the same principal forces. And if we pull aside the spiritual veil on the shore of Gadara, we can see it: Christ and His angels arrayed against Satan and his demons—each striving for the heart and life of a miserable madman. "For we do not wrestle against flesh and blood, but against principalities, against powers, against the rulers of the darkness of this age, against spiritual hosts of wickedness in the heavenly places" (Ephesians 6:12).

When we catch this glimpse of what was happening in the spiritual realm, we can clearly see that this battle is just a microcosm of the greater battle between good and evil that began in heaven.

The Origin of Sin

If you ever find yourself lost in the woods, you would do well to try to retrace your steps to the point where you became lost. Likewise, before we can really understand how the demoniac came to be the host for a legion of unwelcome devils, we need to ask, "Where did the devil come from?"

Did our perfect and holy God create a flawed and wicked devil? Of course not! Rather, God made a splendid, perfect angel named Lucifer, who was the most powerful and beautiful of God's creatures, the highest and brightest of all the angels of heaven. "You were the seal of perfection, full of wisdom and perfect in beauty" (Ezekiel 28:12). But because Lucifer made a series of selfish evil choices, he became a devil. Driven by pride, he chose to become an enemy of God.

Notice how Scripture describes Lucifer, who is now called Satan:

"How you are fallen from heaven, O Lucifer, son of the morning! How you are cut down to the ground, you who weakened the nations! For you have said in your heart: 'I will ascend into heaven, I will exalt my throne above the stars of God; I will also sit on the mount of the congregation on the farthest sides of the north; I will ascend above the heights of the clouds, I will be like the Most High' " (Isaiah 14:12-15).

Lucifer allowed his beauty, intellectual brilliance, and high position to fill him with arrogance. You might even say that the devil's vanity led to his insanity!

Ezekiel 28:12-17 gives some additional insight into his fall:

You were the seal of perfection, full of wisdom and perfect in beauty. You were in Eden, the garden of God; every precious stone was your covering. . . . The workmanship of your timbrels and pipes was prepared for you on the day you were created. You were the anointed cherub who covers; I established you; you were on the holy mountain of God; you walked back and forth in the midst of fiery stones. You were perfect in your ways from the day you were created, till iniquity was found in you. . . . Your heart was lifted up because of your beauty; you corrupted your wisdom for the sake of your splendor.*

---

*The Bible records many other details about Lucifer (see Luke 4:5, 6; 10:18; John 8:44; 2 Peter 2:4; 1 John 3:8; Jude 6; Revelation 12:7-9), but the two passages quoted above are the most complete.

We can only guess as to how long Lucifer served God willingly and with joy before he began to cherish the poisonous seeds of pride in his heart. Perhaps it was for eons. It might be hard to imagine, but if we had known Lucifer before his fall, we would have loved him. Of course, some seem to love him the way he is now!

This naturally raises another question: Did God make a mistake? Was there a glitch in His angel-making factory so that when Lucifer came off the assembly line, he was destined for breakdown?

Not at all! God is perfect, and God is love. I suppose that if He had wanted to, the Lord could have made all of His creatures mere robots. But robots cannot love. Indeed, true love must be freely and willingly given.

So, God took a risk when He bestowed this ability to receive and give love freely. His subjects might end up rejecting His love and rebelling against Him. But God gave the ability anyway. He did so for the same reason that most couples decide to have children even though they know that doing so is a risky business. They bring children into the world despite realizing that they will choose to resist their love. They do so because, like God, they want to share their love.

Here's another question that often raises unnecessary doubts about God: If He is all-powerful, why didn't He just vaporize the wayward angel when he began his revolt?

God allowed Lucifer to carry out his rebellion

for several reasons. First, it helped to settle any potential questions about the freedom of choice God gave His intelligent creatures. Now, no one can say that God forces sentient beings to do anything against their will. They are free to choose their own paths.

Second, God's immediate destruction of Lucifer might have given the other angels serious doubts about His love and government—particularly, those who might have wondered if Satan was actually on to something. God, in wisdom and in love, is allowing the devil to make his point, thereby letting the whole universe see the terrible results.

Third, it would pain a loving God to know that His children obeyed Him only out of a horrifying fear of being exterminated. Like any good parent, He wants His sons and daughters to obey Him because of willing love and good reason rather than from coercion and fear.

Remarkably, in spite of God's patience and goodness, Lucifer refused to repent. Instead, he devised such a cunning rebellion that he managed to recruit one-third of all the angels to join his unholy war against his Creator. Eventually, God cast Lucifer and his followers, now called "devils" and "demons," out of heaven.

War broke out in heaven: Michael and his angels fought with the dragon; and the dragon and his angels fought, but they did not prevail, nor was a place found for them in heaven any longer.

So the great dragon was cast out, that serpent of old, called the Devil, and Satan, who deceives the whole world: he was cast to the earth, and his angels were cast out with him (Revelation 12:7-9).

Fallen but Brilliant

Famous Hollywood women, especially the high-profile movie stars, seem to be instantly recognizable in public. We wonder how they can do simple things, like go to the supermarket, without being swamped by overzealous fans. Most of them manage just fine. How? They have a simple trick: When they don't wear makeup and trendy hairdos, most people don't recognize them. The public has become so familiar with the glamorous but imaginary illusion of who these people are that the real-life stars can circulate among the crowds undetected.

Lucifer has a similar strategy. "Satan . . . transforms himself into an angel of light" (2 Corinthians 11:14). Satan is delighted when people portray him with his stage image. You know the one: the ugly, red, bat-winged creature that is part man and part beast. He loves being pictured as having split hooves, pointed ears, and a long, pointed tail—and don't forget the goatee or that pitchfork he supposedly uses for stoking the fires of hell.

Nothing could be further from the truth. Indeed, such foolish concepts come from a mixture of Greek mythology and medieval art, and absolutely no such nonsense can be found in Scripture. As the quotations above from Isaiah and Ezekiel show, the Bible describes Satan as a brilliant, highly attractive angel with an uncanny ability to communicate. When we realize these characteristics are combined with his devilish designs, we know that we must be very wary.

Satan is a self-proclaimed enemy of God whose aim is to defame His character and capture His kingdom. He also despises you and your loved ones, and he has plans to destroy you because he knows how much God treasures you.

This is why the story of the demoniac demonstrates so well that our only hope is to place our lives in the protective care of our mighty Savior, praying earnestly for His guidance. Without Christ, we are easy prey to Satan's unending attacks, but, as Scripture says, "He who is in you is greater than he who is in the world" (1 John 4:4).

The Bottomless Pit

The first time I toured the famous Carlsbad Caverns in New Mexico, our guide led us by a gaping hole that seems to drop away into endless darkness. It's affectionately called "the bottomless pit." Of course, it isn't really bottomless. In fact, the bottom is only 140 feet down. Apparently, it gets so littered with trash from passersby that rangers have to rappel down into it once a year to pick up the debris.

The Bible speaks of a bottomless pit where Satan will be imprisoned for a millennium. The apostle John wrote:

I saw an angel come down from heaven, having the key of the bottomless pit and a great chain in his hand. And he laid hold of the dragon, that old serpent, which is the Devil, and Satan, and bound him a thousand years, And he cast him into the bottomless pit, and shut him up, and set a seal upon him, that he should deceive the nations no more, till the thousand years should be fulfilled: and after that he must be loosed a little season (Revelation 20:1-3, KJV).

This prophecy will find its fulfillment immediately following the second coming of Jesus. It speaks of a fate that causes every devil to tremble.

The biblical expression "bottomless pit" is a translation of the Greek word *abussos*, from which we get the word "abyss." This word appears also in the story of the demoniac. There the demons beg Jesus "not [to] command them to go out into the abyss" (Luke 8:31).

So, what is this bottomless pit, this abyss that the devils dread? It's a symbol. No one can escape from a bottomless pit. The pit, then, represents the condition Lucifer and his angels will find themselves in when they are bound on earth during the millennium, the thousand years about which Revelation 20 tells us. During that time, there'll be no one alive on earth for the devils to tempt. Those who have accepted God's salvation will have been taken to heaven, and unrepentant sinners will have died at Jesus' second coming (see 1 Thessalonians 4:16, 17; Revelation 19:18, 21).

During this protracted period, Satan and his minions will be "chained in darkness," bound by the circumstances of having nobody to tempt or manipulate. Scripture says God won't spare the angels who sinned, but will deliver them "into chains of darkness, to be reserved for judgment" (2 Peter 2:4; cp. Jude 6). It is perfect torment for workaholic devils to have nothing to do, which is why the demoniac devils were so upset. "They cried out, saying, 'What have we to do with You, Jesus, You Son of God? Have You come here to torment us before the time?' " (Matthew 8:29). They were concerned that Jesus would chain them before God's timetable as revealed in the Bible actually calls for it.

Note this, too: People often treat others the way they feel they should be treated. Jesus said, "When an unclean spirit goes out of a man, he goes through dry places, seeking rest" (Luke 11:24). This "dryness" is a symbol of the absence of God's Spirit, which is why David said, "The rebellious dwell in a dry land" (Psalm 68:6). Perhaps Satan and his devils had this man in chains because they know they're fated to end up in a dry, desolate place devoid of God. "His own iniquities entrap the wicked man, and he is caught in the cords of his sin" (Proverbs 5:22).

Serpent Phobia

Four times in just one year, John Fretwell's air-conditioning equipment company in Dallas was robbed. So, Fretwell went on a snake hunt in Oklahoma and brought back what might be the ultimate in burglar protection: seven diamondback rattle-snakes.

Now, he displays the snakes in the window of his business office, with a sign that says: DANGER: SNAKES BITE. Before going home at night, he frees the five-foot rattlers to glide around the premises. In the morning, armed with a hooked stick and a burlap bag, he rounds them up. The seven rattlers seem to be warding off the burglars. Most people find these stealthy reptiles revolting and terrifying.

Few people relish the idea of studying snakes.* The subject might not sound very appealing; however, Scripture makes these cold-blooded, legless reptiles a symbol of Satan, so it's profitable for us to consider what they reveal about him.

Of course, we know that the first time the devil communicated with the human race was through the medium of a serpent (see Genesis 3:1). This naturally forged a permanent association of Satan with the serpent. Hence, the symbol stuck all the way to Revelation 20:2, KJV, where he is identified as "the dragon, that old serpent, which is the Devil, and Satan."

Snakes have mastered virtually every environment on earth. You will find them in the sea, on land,

---

*My mother was so deathly afraid of snakes that she would jump and scream even when she saw one on television. My brother and I would sometimes capitalize on her phobia by placing a rubber snake in her dresser drawer and enjoying a cruel laugh when she discovered it.

under the ground, and in trees. There are even a few varieties that can sail through the air. Satan has adapted his enticements to tempt every person in almost any environment.

The benefits to understanding snakes are great. When I lived in the desert mountains as a young man, rattlesnakes were abundant. A basic knowledge about their habits and behavior helped me avoid ever being bitten, despite several close encounters.

Perhaps this is the reason Jesus commands us to be "wise as serpents, and harmless as doves" (Matthew 10:16). To be as "wise as serpents" and avoid being bitten, we must understand at least a few basics about our clever enemy.

Camouflage and Counterfeits

The Bible says, "The serpent was more subtil than any beast of the field which the Lord God had made" (Genesis 3:1, KJV). Snakes are the ultimate experts in camouflage. Whether hiding in the grass or entwined in the branches of a tree, they are masters of blending into the scenery to remain undetected.

More than that, they are also experts in counterfeiting creatures that are more dangerous. For example, when threatened, the harmless bull snake will vibrate its tail in the dry leaves to mimic the sound of his venomous cousin, the rattler.

For every good creation of God, even love, Satan has a convincing counterfeit. For instance, in the Exodus story, Pharaoh's magicians were frequently able to counterfeit the power and miracles of God (Exodus 7:10-12). Likewise, Satan is most dangerous and effective when he is imitating God's miracles and messengers. Scripture warns about "the spirits of demons, performing signs" (Revelation 16:14).

It's Satan's penchant for deceit that makes God's job complicated. Unlike God, who works only within the confines of truth and respect, Satan will cook up a stew of truth and lies in whatever combination will work best to destroy the lives of those he seeks to manipulate.

This is especially frightening for God's church, because the devil appears to be most lethal when he masquerades as a spiritual being working inside the church. Jesus warned, "Beware of false prophets, who come to you in sheep's clothing, but inwardly they are ravenous wolves" (Matthew 7:15). Satan knows the Bible thoroughly, and he quotes and misquotes passages at the drop of a hat to achieve his ends (see, for example, Matthew 4).

The Sword and the Serpent

Since Satan uses even the Bible in his attempts to trap us, obviously, our only protection lies in knowing God's Word, in storing His truths deep within our minds. David said, "Thy word have I hid in mine heart, that I might not sin against thee" (Psalm 119:11, KJV). The New Testament says, "The word of God is living and powerful, and sharper than any two-edged sword" (Hebrews 4:12). Jesus used this sword to fight off the devil when He was tempted in the desert, and it's still needed and available today.

Satan posed the first question found in Scripture. He asked it in an attempt to discredit God's Word: "Hath God said?" (Genesis 3:1, KJV). From that first insidious query to the present, Satan has ever been seeking to undermine the faith of God's children by casting suspicion on God's Word. Sin, suffering, and death entered the world when Satan succeeded in leading our first parents to doubt and disbelieve God's truth. Planting seeds of skepticism regarding the dependability of Scripture remains the devil's primary war tactic.

This is exactly what Jesus faced when, starving and tempted, He combated the archvillain in the wilderness. But He deflected every assault with Scripture. He "[put] on the whole armor of God" and so was "able to stand against the wiles of the devil" (Ephesians 6:11). Paul continues this thought by counseling us to "take the . . . sword of the Spirit, which is the word of God" (verse 17).

Indeed, the serpent trembles when God's people take hold of the living sword of His Word and turn it against him. Victory comes to God's children when they claim and believe the powerful promises in the Word, "that through these you may be partakers of the divine nature, having escaped the corruption that is in the world through lust" (2 Peter 1:4).

Every Serpent Can Be Beaten

Some wit has said, "Adam blamed Eve, Eve blamed the serpent, and the serpent didn't have a leg to stand on." The account of that first temptation on this planet does focus on the serpent and Eve. Correspondingly, we find the first prophecy pictures an ongoing battle between the woman—who ultimately represents God's church—and the serpent (see Genesis 3:14, 15). This prophecy promises the ultimate victory of the woman's seed, the coming Savior, who would kill the serpent. In verse 15, God, speaking to the serpent, says, "I will put enmity between you and the woman, and between your seed and her Seed; He shall bruise your head, and you shall bruise His heel."

Notice that the serpent bites the heel of the woman's seed, not the toe. The heel is the back of the foot, the lowest part of the body. Satan gets us from behind, when we are at our lowest point. He came to tempt Jesus when He was weak and tired after forty days of fasting.

The good news is that Satan only manages to bruise the heel of Christ and the church, which continues to limp along despite the injury. On the other hand, the serpent receives a mortal wound to the head, promising the ultimate victory of Jesus over the devil.

When the Lord commissioned Moses to return to Egypt and lead His people to freedom, He gave him a strange sign. God told him to take his shepherd's rod and " 'cast it on the ground.' So he cast it on the ground, and it became a serpent; and Moses fled from it. Then the Lord said to Moses, 'Reach out your hand and take it by the tail' (and he reached out his hand and caught it, and it became a rod in his hand)" (Exodus 4:3, 4).

In the Bible, a rod is a symbol of power and protection (see Revelation 12:5; Psalm 23:4). The changing of Moses' rod into a serpent signaled to Moses that God would give him power over and protection from the forces of evil as he ventured into the snake pit of Pharaoh's palace. God has promised this same power to all of His children who seek to work with Jesus to liberate others from slavery to Satan. Jesus confirmed this: "Behold, I give unto you power to tread on serpents and scorpions, and over all the power of the enemy: and nothing shall by any means hurt you" (Luke 10:19). More on this in the next section!

Flying Serpents

Dozens of cultures have legends and traditions about flying serpents or dragons. These can be seen the world over in ancient carvings and art. Fables are often rooted in some element of truth. For example, there is a snake in the tropical rainforests that can spring from a tree, flatten its ribcage, and glide a short distance—something like what a flying squirrel does.

Beyond this modern example, many Bible commentators believe that at one time snakes had wings and could fly. The fossil record is full of examples of flying reptiles, like the pterodactyl that lived before the Flood. Moreover, the Bible itself alludes to the existence of flying serpents. One prophecy says, "Out of the serpent's roots will come forth a viper, and its offspring will be a fiery flying serpent" (Isaiah 14:29). Genesis 3:14 explains why we do not see flying snakes of this sort today: "The Lord God said to the serpent: 'Because you have done this, you are cursed more than all cattle, and more than every beast of the field; on your belly you shall go, and you shall eat dust all the days of your life.' "

If part of the serpent's punishment for tempting Eve was that from then on it must travel on its belly, it is clear that before the curse, it propelled itself differently. Satan is called "the prince of the power of the air" (Ephesians 2:2). Just as the curse grounded the serpent, Lucifer's wings were clipped when he was cast to the earth (see Revelation 12).

Furthermore, because snakes do not rely on energy from food to generate body heat, they can survive on an extremely meager diet. Some wait for months between meals, and a few survive by eating a single, large meal just once or twice a year. Likewise, Satan has perfected the art of patiently waiting for his prey to relax its guard so he can devour it.

It's Not Wise to Play With Snakes

A young man in Orlando, Florida, was nearly killed by his pet anaconda. He had owned the snake for many years and had always felt comfortable allowing the creature to coil around his arms and neck. Somehow, though, he hadn't noticed that what was once a manageable, six-foot-long novelty had become a sixteen-foot-long monster.

One day, while this young man was demonstrating to friends the confidence he had in his pet, the constrictor began to squeeze his neck and chest. After a desperate struggle, the man's friends and his knife-wielding mother were able to force the creature to release his prey. The man barely survived.

Some people have convinced themselves that it's safe to communicate with Satan or even to debate the devil. However, the fate of Eve when she fell into the hands of the enemy illustrates well that this is a big mistake. We should never toy with temptation— even the "littlest" of sins can be deadly.*

When we depend upon our own wisdom, we're no match against the evil genius of the great serpent. But through Christ, we can stomp the head of this sinister snake. Jesus was speaking of this power over evil when He said, "These signs will follow those who believe: In My name . . . they will take up serpents" (Mark 16:17, 18).

Some misguided pastors have interpreted this passage to mean that Christians should double as snake charmers—that they should prove their faith by handling rattlesnakes or other venomous vipers. For obvious reasons, the membership in these congregations has always remained small. The New Testament account of Paul's shipwreck reveals how to understand this passage correctly:

The natives showed us unusual kindness; for they kindled a fire and made us all welcome,

---

*A rattlesnake only two minutes old can strike effectively! During a picnic, a two-year-old uncovered a brood of baby rattlesnakes. The unsuspecting child began to play with what she thought were pretty worms. She was bitten repeatedly and didn't survive. Likewise, some people feel that little sins are harmless, but in the end they prove fatal more often than do the more obvious, "big" transgressions.

because of the rain that was falling and because of the cold. But when Paul had gathered a bundle of sticks and laid them on the fire, a viper came out because of the heat, and fastened on his hand. So when the natives saw the creature hanging from his hand, they said to one another, "No doubt this man is a murderer, whom, though he has escaped the sea, yet justice does not allow to live." But he shook off the creature into the fire and suffered no harm. However, they were expecting that he would swell up or suddenly fall down dead. But after they had looked for a long time and saw no harm come to him, they changed their minds and said that he was a god (Acts 28:1-6).

As God saved Paul from the venom of that serpent, He will save us from the poison of sin. "You shall tread upon the lion and the cobra, the young lion and the serpent you shall trample underfoot" (Psalm 91:13). However, we are never to deliberately seek out snakes to flirt with disaster. That would be tempting the Lord (see Matthew 4:7).

Snake on a Stick

One of the most well-known, beloved, and memorized verses in the Bible is John 3:16, which reads: "God so loved the world that He gave His only begotten Son, that whoever believes in Him should not perish but have everlasting life." But if you were to ask people—even Christians—to quote the two verses that precede this one, I would venture that not one in fifty could do it! Yet verse 16 is actually the continuation of a thought begun before it. Here are the verses when read together:

> As Moses lifted up the serpent in the wilderness, even so must the Son of Man be lifted up, that whoever believes in Him should not perish but have eternal life. For God so loved the world that He gave His only begotten Son, that whoever believes in Him should not perish but have everlasting life (John 3:14-16).

It's interesting to consider that just before John 3:16 we read about the serpent. In fact, these three verses together encapsulate the entire great controversy between the serpent and our Lord. Let's look at the Old Testament story to which Jesus was alluding in the Gospel of John:

> The people spoke against God and against Moses: "Why have you brought us up out of Egypt to die in the wilderness? For there is no food and no water, and our soul loathes this worthless bread." So the Lord sent fiery serpents among the people, and they bit the people; and many of the people of Israel died (Numbers 21:5, 6).

Remember that sin entered the world when the serpent succeeded in tempting our first parents to doubt God's word. In this story, after the children of Israel rejected God's bread (a symbol for Jesus and the Word), the serpents bit them.* Let's read on:

> Therefore the people came to Moses, and said, "We have sinned, for we have spoken against the Lord and against you; pray to the Lord that He take away the serpents from us." So Moses prayed for the people. Then the Lord said to Moses, "Make a fiery serpent, and set it on a pole; and it shall be that everyone who is bitten, when he looks at it, shall live." So Moses made a bronze serpent, and put it on a pole; and so it was, if a serpent had bitten anyone, when he looked at the bronze serpent, he lived" (Numbers 21:7-9).

For a nation of shepherds, this serpent raised on a pole served as a strong symbol that each of them understood well. Snakes are a deadly menace to sheep and goats. A dog might survive a rattlesnake bite without any specialized treatment, but sheep and goats are much more fragile. This is one of the reasons why shepherds must carry a rod.† Thus, to the

---

*Since repetition can be helpful, I'll repeat here that it is the Word of God that keeps people from sin (see Psalm 119:11).

†When I lived in the desert, I carried a snake stick that served a couple of purposes. If I found a venomous intruder in my cave, I would "bruise his head" by clubbing it. But a mortally wounded snake might continue to thrash and writhe for hours, and it still has the capacity to strike. So rather than risk grabbing it with my bare hand, I would lift it up with the rod to move it far from my premises.

Jews, a snake on a stick vividly symbolized a defeated serpent. Beyond this, however, the symbol had a much richer prophetic significance.

All who have ever lived upon the earth have felt the deadly sting of "that old serpent, called the Devil . . ." (Revelation 12:9). The fatal effects of sin can be removed only by the provision that God has made. The Israelites saved their lives by looking in faith upon the uplifted serpent. They lived because they believed God's word, and trusted in the means provided for their recovery. So the sinner may look to Christ, and live. He receives pardon through faith in the atoning sacrifice. Unlike the inert and lifeless symbol, Christ has power and virtue in Himself to heal the repenting sinner.*

In short, as Jesus said, "I, if I be lifted up from the earth, will draw all peoples to myself" (John 12:32). A much-loved and well-respected book on the life of Christ says:

The people well knew that in itself the serpent had no power to help them. It was a symbol of Christ. As the image made in the likeness of the destroying serpents was lifted up for their healing, so One made "in the likeness

---

*Ellen G. White, *Patriarchs and Prophets* (Nampa, Idaho: Pacific Press, 1913), 431.

of sinful flesh" (Romans 8:3) was to be their Redeemer.*

As John 12:32 says, it is when we look to Jesus on the cross that we are drawn to Him by His love for us. When we gaze in faith at our Redeemer's sacrifice for us, we are saved from the sting of the serpent and the power of his venom is neutralized—just as the story of the Jews affirms.

Notice that in this Bible story, God did not take away the serpents. Instead, He provided the remedy. As long as we are in this world, we will always have the devil to contend with. However, in the blood of Jesus, God has provided us an abundance of antivenom to save us from the viper's bite! When Jesus was on the cross, although that old serpent, the devil, painfully bruised His "heel," Jesus mortally crushed the serpent's head, smiting it with the rod of Jesse (see Isaiah 11:1).

In the Topkapi Museum in Istanbul, Turkey, a very precious goblet stands in a prominent place. A gold serpent is poised in the very center of the cup. It is decorated with ruby eyes and diamond fangs, its mouth is open, and it looks like it's ready to strike. When the goblet is filled with wine, the red liquid hides the snake; but as the wine is drunk, the serpent, with its menacing appearance, is revealed.

---

*Ellen G. White, *The Desire of Ages* (Nampa, Idaho: Pacific Press, 1940), 174.

When Jesus came to die for us, He shrank from the thought of bearing our sin and the separation from the Father that would entail. That's why He prayed, "O My Father, if it is possible, let this cup pass from Me; nevertheless, not as I will, but as You will" (Matthew 26:39). Then, humbling Himself, Jesus drank the cup of sin down to the dregs. And while He was raised on the cross, the serpent, who had been enjoying every lash and insult Jesus suffered, struck with all of his diabolical vengeance.

Yet Jesus bore it all.

Good-Luck Charms

All snakes are cold-blooded creatures that depend on outside sources for heat and cooling. They are also "cold-blooded" regarding their offspring. After baby snakes are born, or hatched, the parents generally abandon them. In some cases, they even devour them. Satan has roughly the same level of warmth, compassion, and loyalty for those who serve him. He is the heartless, cold-blooded epitome of evil.

The bronze serpent Moses forged and elevated on the stick somehow managed to survive all the wanderings and battles of the Israelites for more than seven hundred years. Most of the surrounding pagan nations worshiped serpents as gods of fertility and mystical power, and over time, the Israelites began to imitate their neighbors. They were soon treating the bronze relic of God's forgiveness as a deity in and of itself (see 2 Kings 18:3, 4).

BROKEN CHAINS

Like these ancient Israelites, millions of souls around the world today are inadvertently worshiping the serpent while thinking they are worshiping the Lord. They have slowly, unwittingly, been seduced into base idolatry. Furthermore, many Christians have sadly adopted this same practice, treating the symbol of the cross much like the bronze serpent of the ancient Jews.

However, just as the Israelites were not to worship the serpent on the pole, we are not to bow down or to pray before a cross. Neither are we commanded to make the sign of the cross on our persons. Indeed, there is no mystical power or virtue in this image of an ancient torture implement! "Jesus said to His disciples, 'If anyone desires to come after Me, let him deny himself, and take up his cross, and follow Me' " (Matthew 16:24). He was commanding His followers to *bear* the cross, not to *wear* the cross. Revelation says we are saved not by the cross but by the blood of Jesus. It was the cross as a reminder of Jesus' love and sacrifice that Paul and the other apostles exalted, not the revolting instrument itself. "He humbled Himself and became obedient to the point of death, even the death of the cross" (Philippians 2:8).

So, it is the redemption provided on the cross on which Christians should focus. Hebrews 12:2 says it perfectly: "Looking unto Jesus, the author and finisher of our faith, who for the joy that was set before Him endured the cross, despising the shame."

The Devil's Demise

A newspaper in Texas reported that a taxidermist was bitten by a frozen rattlesnake. Robert Herndon buys poisonous rattlers, freezes them to death, and markets the preserved remains. He usually tapes their mouths before he starts cutting into them, but he apparently skipped the tape that time. So, again, the warning proved true: "Never assume a poisonous snake is dead."

Some people have wondered, "If Jesus defeated Satan at the crucifixion, why do we still see and feel so much evidence of his evil activity?"

The devil knows he was defeated at the cross, but he is also completely crazed with pride and anger. So that he can inflict as much heartache on God as possible, he continues to fight tenaciously, wanting to take down with him as many as possible. "The devil has come down to you, having great wrath, because he knows that he has a short time" (Revelation 12:12). Satan is now thrashing about wildly in his final death throes, striking at anyone still within his reach.

When Robinson Crusoe's good man Friday asked him why God didn't do something about the devil, Crusoe gave him the right answer. He said, "God will destroy him." The Bible promises that Satan will ultimately be destroyed for his deadly rebellion.

In the story of the demoniac, the demon-filled swine drowned in the lake. The Bible promises that, ultimately, Satan and his angels will meet a similar fate. They'll be cast into the lake of fire. "The devil, who deceived them, was cast into the lake of fire and brimstone" (Revelation 20:10). In a prophecy of the devil's end, Ezekiel wrote:

> I will cast thee to the ground; I will lay thee before kings, that they may behold thee. Thou hast defiled thy sanctuaries by the multitude of thine iniquities, by the iniquity of thy traffic; therefore will I bring forth a fire from the midst of thee, it shall devour thee, and I will bring thee to ashes upon the earth in the sight of all them that behold thee. All they that know thee among the people shall be astonished at thee: thou shalt be a terror, and never shalt thou be any more (Ezekiel 28:17-19, KJV).*

This frightening doom also holds true for those here on earth who follow the devil. "He [Christ] will also say to those on the left hand, 'Depart from Me, you cursed, into the everlasting fire prepared for the devil and his angels' " (Matthew 25:41).

An enemy terrorist has kidnapped this planet. But Jesus came to pay the ransom and destroy the archterrorist. "For this purpose the Son of God was manifested, that He might destroy the works of the devil" (1 John 3:8). Matthew 23:33 echoes, "Serpents, brood of vipers! How can you escape the condemnation of hell?"

---

*Isaiah 14:15 also foretells of the devil, "You shall be brought down to Sheol, to the lowest depths of the Pit."

The good news is that in heaven, we will no longer need to walk in fear. Isaiah 11:8, 9 describes a paradise without harmful snakes—or devils:

> The sucking child shall play on the hole of the asp, and the weaned child shall put his hand on the cockatrice' [viper's] den. They shall not hurt nor destroy in all my holy mountain: for the earth shall be full of the knowledge of the LORD, as the waters cover the sea (KJV).

A Lion With a Plan

Every year, Butte, Montana, hosts an amazing ice-sculpting competition. Every artist is given a large block of solid ice. As the sculptors begin chiseling on their fresh block of frozen water, they have a blueprint in their minds of what the final work will be. One might choose to chisel a dragon, another might sculpt an angel—but all of them have an ultimate plan in mind.

The Bible isn't content to identify Satan with a serpent—it also compares his tactics to those of a lion. "Be sober, be vigilant; because your adversary the devil walks about like a roaring lion, seeking whom he may devour." (1 Peter 5:8).

Lions use craftiness and diversion to capture their prey. Like the devil, they spring suddenly and unexpectedly upon their victims and care nothing about their prey's suffering. And lions always seem to have a plan for taking down their targets in the quickest manner possible.

BROKEN CHAINS

Most people recognize that God has a plan for their lives, but I am frequently met with troubled and bewildered stares when I ask, "Do you know that the devil has a plan for your life?" It's true. And the horror of it is that the devil's ultimate plan for you is the same as the one he had for the demoniac!

As far as possible, the devil wants to erase the image of God from the mind of his prey using any means possible—including disguising himself. Unwisely, and unbiblically, many assume Satan will openly appear as God's enemy in the end-time, but this is far from reality. Although Satan is indeed God's bitterest enemy, he will fake being righteous (see Matthew 24:24). He will appear as a glorious, angelic being and will seek the worship of the masses (see 2 Corinthians 11:13-15; Revelation 13:12).

Scripture is clear that his godly appearance will be so convincing that virtually "all the world" will wonder after the beast (Revelation 13:3). Even God's children are nearly deceived (see Matthew 24:24). We can safely resist Satan only by first giving our hearts to God and trusting completely in His Word! "Submit to God. Resist the devil and he will flee from you. Draw near to God and He will draw near to you" (James 4:7, 8).

The incredible deliverance of the demoniac highlights the two great blueprints for every person's life. It is a vivid display of what God has planned for humanity and what the devil would do to God's creatures.

Jesus reveals the perfect image of God; the lunatic, the image of Lucifer. And every day, little by little, we are being transformed into the image of the master we decide to follow. The way we choose to respond to the trials and temptations that come each day determines our choice. But we must remember that Jesus is by far a stronger master; we can rely on Him for victory. " 'Not by might nor by power, but by My Spirit,' says the Lord of hosts" (Zechariah 4:6).

Most people would never be foolish enough to fight a grown lion with their bare hands. But Samson and David were able to slay lions when the Spirit of God came upon them. It is only by the power of God's Spirit that we can resist the devil. Psalm 91:13 declares, "You shall tread upon the lion and the cobra, the young lion and the serpent you shall trample underfoot."

A Cosmic Contrast

Just before the first bell of a boxing match, the boxers generally stand in the middle of the ring while the referee reviews with them the rules of engagement. The tension is often electric as the audience watches the two opponents face off, staring at each other. Sometimes one of them will glare with anger or flash a sarcastic smile, while others exude a calm, knowing confidence.

The story of the demoniac is the story of a big fight. In the end-time scenario, it's just before the "main event." The principal fighters have battled before, during the war in heaven. This is a cosmic rematch on an isolated, beachside ring on earth.

In one corner we see Jesus, the Prince of light—the perfect reflection of the Father. God's plan is for every soul to reflect Jesus—that's why He became a man. In the other corner, we have the raving demoniac, the devil's ultimate plan for every soul. It's an amazing scene, and if we could peer behind the spiritual veil, we would see an audience of angels—some fallen, some holy—cheering for their respective leaders.

Amazingly, this is the only place where the Bible pictures Jesus engaging in any form of conversation with demons. He did it to help us realize the tremendous significance of this experience. The armies of heaven and hell were arrayed against one another on that beach, fighting over the soul of that desperate man. And Jesus meant for us to see these two sides competing for your soul every day, because we need to see how different they really are.

To look at it from a slightly different perspective, award-winning photography is a combination of framing, focus, composition, light, and perfect timing. The story of the demoniac is the ultimate photograph; Scripture depicts no greater contrast.

Jesus is the sum total of everything good; He is filled with God. "In Him dwells all the fullness of the Godhead bodily" (Colossians 2:9). By contrast, the demoniac was the epitome of badness; he was filled with demons!* So many, in fact, that there's no other instance in the Bible of anyone possessed by anywhere near this number of demons.

Incarnation is our term for God's becoming a man in the person of Jesus. The demoniac is the closest thing we see in the Bible to the incarnation of Satan. So, in this story we have a freeze-frame of God becoming a man to save a man who had become a devil!

These two leaders can also be said to represent the trees in the Garden of Eden. Jesus was the tree of life, and the devil, in the form of the demoniac, was the tree of death. These two trees put out two different kinds of fruit. Eating from Jesus' tree, we fill our lives with God's plan and take on the mind of Jesus. We walk in His steps, do His good works, and enjoy "the fruit of the Spirit [which are] love, joy, peace, longsuffering, kindness, goodness, faithfulness, gentleness, self-control" (Galatians 5:22, 23; see also Philippians 2:5; John 20:21; 1 Peter 2:21; 1 John 2:6).

But eating from the devil's tree, we are filled with "adultery, fornication, uncleanness, lewdness, idolatry, sorcery, hatred, contentions, jealousies, outbursts of wrath, selfish ambitions, dissensions, heresies,

---

*Throughout Rome's history, the number of soldiers in a legion varied between 4,500 and 6,000. Sometimes there were more. Bible commentator Matthew Henry said, "What multitudes of fallen spirits there must be, and all enemies to God and man, when here was a legion in one poor wretched creature!"

envy, murders, drunkenness, revelries, and the like; of which I tell you beforehand, just as I also told you in time past, that those who practice such things will not inherit the kingdom of God" (Galatians 5:19, 20). The madman modeled perfectly this destructive plan of the devil.

What fighter will you back? What picture do you want to look at? What tree will you eat from? If we choose the right one, we're promised that we will speak with God face to face and see him eye to eye.

The Sin of the Devil Is Our Own

A man from the town of Grand Forks, North Dakota, traveled to Fargo to rob the First Community Bank. He scribbled a note demanding money and gave it to the teller. Frightened, she gave the man what he asked for and watched him run out the door. Police searches of the surrounding area turned up nothing. But upon reviewing the robber's note, the police discovered he had written his note on his own bank deposit slip, which of course had his name and address! The police arrested the robber on his front porch.

Sin makes us do crazy things and, let's face it, some very dumb things too. I once saw a bumper sticker that read, "Insanity is hereditary—you get it from your children." In reality, we are all born with the seeds of insanity. I was once told that people in psychiatric hospitals use the words *I, me, my, mine,* and *myself* ten times more frequently than those who are considered sane. It's a practical illustration that selfishness and sin breed insanity. It so happens that the Bible also teaches us about the only antidote: "The fear of the Lord is the beginning of wisdom: a good understanding have all those who do His commandments" (Psalm 111:10).

There is little doubt that this demoniac was not born in the depraved condition in which we found him, so naturally we have to wonder, "How did this man get this way?" The story of King Nebuchadnezzar, found in Daniel 5, contains one clue. Unrestrained pride and sensuality led the Babylonian monarch to a state of animalistic insanity.

Pride, of course, was the sin that led to the devil's fall. It is an attitude that accompanies almost every other sin too. We find it also in the story of King Saul. It ultimately led him to a brooding demonic depression.

The state of Illinois gets its name from an Indian word that means "tribe of superior men." I don't imagine that present-day residents of that state ordinarily boast of themselves as superior, but throughout history, many have regarded themselves as superior to others. One of the worst examples, of course, comes from Nazi Germany, where Hitler taught that the Aryan Germans and related peoples were a superior race. Here's an instance in which the spirit of pride led an entire nation into beastlike sin.

The Bible urges us not to think more highly of ourselves than we ought. It also asks that we honor others above ourselves (see Romans 12:10). "Pride goes before destruction, and a haughty spirit before a fall. Better to be of a humble spirit with the lowly, than to divide the spoil with the proud" (Proverbs 16:18, 19).

The devil is not impersonal, like a statue. Rather, he is the passionate antithesis of all that God is. While Jesus is meek and humble, pride has driven Satan to a rage. While God is selfless love, the devil is unadulterated selfishness. Jesus is the way, the truth, and the life; the devil is a liar, and his way leads to death. That's why his actions are everything that God would never do, and that's why he resorts to some nasty tricks.

Indeed, you might have heard the story of the unscrupulous lawyer who asked the defendant in a courtroom, "Have you stopped beating your wife?" No matter how the accused answers, he will sound guilty. Similarly, Satan is a master at superimposing his own sick characteristics upon the Lord. When a natural disaster strikes, insurance companies call it an "act of God." But the book of Job teaches that Satan has the power to cause natural disasters.

In the very worst cases, when people see innocent children suffer, they react by shaking their fists at God and calling Him a sadist. The demons in our story reacted this way. They said, "What have I to do with You, Jesus, Son of the Most High God? I implore You by God that You do not *torment* me" (Mark 5:7, emphasis supplied). If we really want to understand God's character, all we have to do is to look at the person of Jesus. He said, "He who has seen Me has seen the Father" (John 14:9). By looking at Him, His humble ways, we will more often deny those selfish passions that draw us to the path of the devil— the path that opens us up to his influence and possession.

Demon Possession in Three Easy Steps

The subjects of devils and demon possession seem fantastic and superstitious to "sophisticated," modern-day Americans. These days, even the most fundamental Christians are inclined to relegate demonic activity to pagan lands and missionary experiences, or to pass it off as a mental disturbance poorly diagnosed by some religious zealot.*

However, Bible-believing Christians have always accepted the notions of demons and their worldwide activity—the New Testament offers ample examples. For instance, John 13:27 says of Judas, "Satan entered him." Even a superficial acceptance of the Bible will compel you to see the reality of demonic activity.

Before moving on, we should probably also understand that there is a big difference between de-

---

*It's true that there have been many cases of people who have had medical conditions, such as epilepsy, who were falsely accused of being demon-possessed. But there also might be far more cases of people who are demon-possessed whose bizarre behavior is seen as medically solvable—often with the result that the demoniac is medicated into a complacent stupor.

mon possession and demon harassment. Everybody's tempted or harassed by the devil. If you don't think you are ever tempted by the devil, it is likely that you are nearly possessed. Only those who are swimming against the current feel the pull of the river. Of course, it's not a sin to be tempted; we sin only when we surrender to temptation.

There is little likelihood that we can attribute the deplorable condition of the crazed man in our story to anything but demon possession. How did he become possessed? Contrary to what *Rosemary's Baby* portrayed, children are not typically born demon possessed. It's also not likely that the demoniac woke up one day and announced, "Hey, I'd like to be demon possessed!" And he probably didn't "come down" with it quickly, as happens with the flu or measles.

Quite the opposite, the devil moves in very slowly and quietly until he can take complete control of his prey—he's the camel working his nose into the tent. As S. D. Gordon opined, "It is startling to think that Satan can actually come into the heart of a man in such close touch with Jesus as Judas was. And more—he is cunningly trying to do it today. Yet he can get in only through a door opened from the inside. Every man controls the door of his own life."*

At some time this man made a conscious decision to be free—not from evil, but from God's influence.

---

*S. D. Gordon, "The Bent-Knee Time," *Christianity Today*, vol. 33, no. 10.

He likely ached to be free from the restrictions and responsibilities of life. He wanted to be free to do what he wanted to do. Satan often uses the idea of being "one's own person" and doing "one's own thing" to tempt people into sin. They want to "be free!"

However, the truth is that when we surrender to sin, we lose control. So, in one sense, yes, the demoniac did become free—no human restraint could hold him. He was no longer bound by social conventions that told him how to dress or how to behave. He was free from societal obligations, because society no longer wanted him. He became totally free. But his freedom cost him more than he could have ever imagined. Sin became his cruel master.

Do you not know that to whom you present yourselves slaves to obey, you are that one's slaves whom you obey, whether of sin leading to death, or of obedience leading to righteousness? But God be thanked that though you were slaves of sin, yet you obeyed from the heart that form of doctrine to which you were delivered. And having been set free from sin, you became slaves of righteousness (Romans 6:16-18).

Thomas Brooks said, "Satan promises the best, but pays with the worst; he promises honor and pays with disgrace; he promises pleasure and pays with pain; he promises profit and pays with loss; he promises life and pays with death."

Satan can't possess us without our help. Demon possession generally takes hold when people, through long and continued submission to the devil's suggestions, lose nearly all of their will and capacity to resist. Their will is no longer their own, just as this madman in manacles was not his own.

Earmarks of Possession

John 8:44 warns sinners, "You are of your father the devil, and the desires of your father you want to do. He was a murderer from the beginning, and does not stand in the truth, because there is no truth in him. When he speaks a lie, he speaks from his own resources, for he is a liar and the father of it."

Can we easily recognize a person who is demon possessed? Obviously, it would be hard for a person to hide possession by six thousand demons. But it makes me shudder to consider how many people we might encounter, day after day, who are possessed by one or two or even a dozen demons—all the while managing to blend undiagnosed right into common society.

There are some telltale signs of which we can be wary. Often, those who are struggling with demonic possession carry with them a dark, depressing cloud that contaminates all those around them. You can almost tell when they enter a room; it's as though their gloomy atmosphere is contagious. But there are several more-tangible indicators, and the demoniac in our story features many of these prominent characteristics.

Radical personality change. The "before and after" of the demoniac's life reveals that he was once a totally different person. This shows that his very identity and individuality were swallowed up by the demons within him.

Those who have witnessed demon possession often report that each demon seems to have its own distinct personality and that the individual possessed often manifests the various personalities of the demon or demons possessing them. The demoniac must have demonstrated a wide array of the ghoulish personalities that were striving for the mastery of his senses.

Antisocial behavior. The conduct of the pathetic lunatic was obviously antisocial, which explains why he was living in the remote solitude of the tombs. Clearly, he lacked all social skills. In many cases, this symptom of demon possession might include lewd or sexually explicit behavior. ("He wore no clothes.")

Spiritual insight. The possessed man also showed an unusual depth of spiritual insight. He recognized Jesus to be God even before Jesus spoke. This insight was obviously beyond any human spiritual capacity. Demons also have an intuitive knowledge of their impending doom. ("Have You come here to torment us before the time?")

Supernatural strength. Normal means of human confinement couldn't control the demoniac. No chain was strong enough—he snapped shackles as if they were strings. Other places in Scripture also associate superhuman strength with demon possession (Acts 19:16).

Torment. The price tag of possession is very high; those who fall victim to demons often suffer constant torment. Such was the case of the demoniac (see Mark 5:5). His animalistic shrieks horrified the locals. Those possessed by demons might also babble incoherently. ("He was crying out.")

Tendency toward self-destruction. Another indicator of demonic possession is the desire to harm one's self. ("Cutting himself with stones.") Other demoniacs described in Scripture were bent on self-destruction, often accompanied by fits and convulsions (see Mark 9:17-29). The drowning of the swine dramatically demonstrates the self-destructive desires of the demons. We also see this played out in Judas's end. (Remember, Scripture says that at the Last Supper, Satan entered him—see Luke 22:3.) "Then he threw down the pieces of silver in the temple and departed, and went and hanged himself" (Matthew 27:5).

A preoccupation with death. The demon-possessed frequently have a morbid preoccupation with death and its trappings. The demoniac chose to live in a cemetery. Likewise, in our culture today, young people easily become addicted to rock music with suicidal themes. They frequently dress in black clothing and highlight themselves with black or blood-colored lipstick and fingernail polish.*

---

*Of course, neither black nor red are inherently evil.

They also often wear jewelry or sport tattoos that depict skulls and other graveyard images.

Casting Out Stubborn Spirits

After televangelist Jimmy Swaggart was caught in a moral scandal, he defied the orders of the Assemblies of God to refrain from preaching for a year and undergo counseling. Instead, he assured the public that he was free of moral defect. He said Oral Roberts had already cast the demons from his body over the phone. Roberts confirmed the report, insisting that his friend had demons who had embedded their claws deeply in his flesh. Now that the rascals were gone, Swaggart and Roberts asserted, the televangelist could get on with preparing the way for Christ's return. But only a few months later, according to media reports, Swaggart was caught in Palm Springs with a prostitute in his car, which was strewn with pornographic magazines.

I need to tread softly as I venture on the important topic of the casting out of demons. I don't want to leave you with the impression that there's some simple, three-step formula. It would be nice if a doctor could prescribe a pill that would eliminate all of the demons within like medicine that kills worms in a dog. But the casting out of devils is not something to be taken lightly. It certainly involves more than speaking a few mystical words over the phone.

I am very suspicious of Christians who claim to have a special exorcism ministry, because I find no evidence in the Bible that one of the gifts of the Spirit is the casting out of demons.*

However, the Bible plainly teaches that in cases of demon possession, God's servants can, through His power, cast the demons out. We are no match for these spiritual enemies; but in the might of our Lord, we can stand against even legions of them. "Heal the sick, cleanse the lepers, raise the dead, cast out demons. Freely you have received, freely give" (Matthew 10:8).

Still, God's Word cautions that the devil does not go easily. And casting out demons is not a business to be executed with a flippant attitude. Earlier, I alluded to a story in the book of Acts that illustrates just this point. Some presumptuous young men attempted to cast out a demon using some canned formula they thought the apostle Paul was using. Their plan backfired terribly. Let's take look at the whole story:

> Some of the itinerant Jewish exorcists took it upon themselves to call the name of the Lord Jesus over those who had evil spirits, saying, "We exorcise you by the Jesus whom Paul preaches." Also there were seven sons of Sceva, a Jewish chief priest, who did so. And the evil spirit answered and said, "Jesus I know, and Paul

---

*Nor do I believe that we should seek out people who are demon-possessed or who print business cards that advertise "Demons 'R Us." I believe that patronizing such people borders on looking for trouble and tempting the Lord.

I know; but who are you?" Then the man in whom the evil spirit was leaped on them, overpowered them, and prevailed against them, so that they fled out of that house naked and wounded (Acts 19:13-16).

Satan clings tenaciously to his victims. The story of the Exodus tells us that Moses, like Jesus, came to save his people from slavery. The pharaoh, like Satan, fiercely resisted freeing them from their bondage, even though it meant the destruction of his kingdom. Indeed, new birth always has some element of pain and blood. Freedom from tyranny often requires sacrifice and struggle—whether it is the birth of the nation or of a single soul as it is being liberated from the shackles of sin.

What Can We Do?

Cite Scripture. When Jesus battled with the devil in the wilderness, He quoted Scripture. It's our most powerful weapon. We must plunge the sword of God's Word directly into the temptations of the deceiver. It was frequently in the context of preaching that Jesus cast out devils: "He was preaching in their synagogues throughout all Galilee, and casting out demons" (Mark 1:39). Encourage those who are afflicted to read the Bible, and, if they can, to attend services where the Word is proclaimed. You might even read Scripture aloud to them.

Pray and fast. Once, a father brought his son to Jesus and complained about a demon that possessed his boy: "Wherever it seizes him, it throws him down; he foams at the mouth, gnashes his teeth, and becomes rigid. So I spoke to Your disciples, that they should cast him out, but they could not" (Mark 9:18).

Jesus responded, "This kind can come out by nothing but prayer and fasting" (Mark 9:29). It might require several sessions, or even days, of special prayer and fasting to see a soul delivered. Don't give up easily; you can be sure the devil won't.

Believe. We must pray in faith that God will liberate those who are tormented. Jesus said, "If you can believe, all things are possible to him who believes" (Mark 9:23).

Prepare your own heart. Those involved in praying should search their own souls and confess and forsake their sins. "Brethren, if a man is overtaken in any trespass, you who are spiritual restore such a one in a spirit of gentleness, considering yourself lest you also be tempted" (Galatians 6:1).

Anoint with oil. Often there is a thin line between medical and spiritual affliction, between physiological and diabolical torment. For this reason, it might be appropriate to anoint the victim with oil. "Is anyone among you sick? Let him call for the elders of the church, and let them pray over him, anointing him with oil in the name of the Lord. And the prayer of faith will save the sick, and the Lord will raise him up. And if he has committed sins, he will be forgiven" (James 5:14, 15).

Invoke Jesus' name. Always invoke the name and authority of Jesus when venturing into spiritual combat. "Paul, greatly annoyed, turned and said to the spirit, 'I command you in the name of Jesus Christ to come out of her.' And he came out that very hour." (Acts 16:18). "These signs will follow those who believe: In My name they will cast out demons" (Mark 16:17).

Does the Devil Know Your Name?

Sports enthusiasts might know the names of all the players on their favorite team. But only a few unusually gifted athletes become household names among average citizens—names like *Michael Jordan, Babe Ruth, Mohammed Ali,* and *Tiger Woods.* During World War II, every Japanese soldier recognized the name of General Douglas MacArthur.

This also holds true in the spiritual realm. Wherever Jesus went throughout His earthly ministry, the devils He encountered always knew who He was. "There was a man in their synagogue with an unclean spirit. And he cried out, saying, 'Let us alone! What have we to do with You, Jesus of Nazareth? Did You come to destroy us? I know who You are— the Holy One of God!' " (Mark 1:23, 24). Another time we learn, "He healed many who were sick with various diseases, and cast out many demons; and He did not allow the demons to speak, because they knew Him" (Mark 1:34). This awareness is understandable. After all, Jesus had once been their heavenly commander.

God, of course, is omniscient; He knows all things. He knows even more than just our names—He knows the very number of hairs we have on our heads! The devil, on the other hand, is not all knowing. However, he is acquainted with certain people because he regards their godly reputation and conduct as a threat. A perfect example of this is Job, who apparently was a big thorn in the devil's side.

Scripture recounts, "The Lord said to Satan, 'Have you considered My servant Job, that there is none like him on the earth, a blameless and upright man, one who fears God and shuns evil?' " (Job 1:8). The devil responded that he was well acquainted with Job. And you can be sure that the devil also knew the names *Moses, Noah, Daniel,* and *David.* And the enemies of God knew Paul well: "The evil spirit answered and said, 'Jesus I know, and Paul I know; but who are you?' " (Acts 19:15).

Does the devil know who you are? It's a disturbing question, but one worth considering. I'm sure it might even make you shudder, because nobody wants to invite the diabolical attention of Lucifer. Still, wouldn't we want to live a life that alarms the enemy?

I submit that when we consecrate our lives to God and live that way, we become a threat to the devil. Whether we like it or not, we are all players on a cosmic football field, surrounded by the angels of God and Satan—all watching from their stadium seats. The angels of God certainly cheer our victories, and the demons obviously boo. And when we publicly announce our faith in Christ's promises, our names are proclaimed over the cosmic sound system. "I say to you, whoever confesses Me before men, him the Son of Man also will confess before the angels of God" (Luke 12:8).

On the other hand, when we deny Christ by our words and behavior, demons cheer while God's angels hang their heads and fold their wings in despair. " 'He who denies Me [Jesus] before men will be denied before the angels of God' " (Luke 12:9). So fight valiantly for victory on the field of life that your Master may pronounce with beaming smile, "Well done good and faithful servant" (Matthew 25:23).

In the next section we'll see how the Lord will help you do all this and more . . .

The Divine Deliverance

Part 1: Finding God's Forgiveness

"When he saw Jesus from afar, he ran and worshiped Him."
—Mark 5:6

Coming From Afar

On August 27, 2003, Mars nearly caught up with the earth, passing within a mere 34,649,589 miles of our planet. That was Mars's closest approach ever in recorded history. The red planet won't come that close again until 2287.

For several nights during that period, Mars was the second brightest object in the night sky (the moon being the first). That month, I spent several nights on the porch with my family, gazing at the clear heavens. I remember being deeply impressed with the immensity of the universe.

Our planet is so small—it is less than the smallest grain of sand on the endless beach of space. It would have been so easy for God to snap His fingers and obliterate this rebellious little atom we call home.

Have you ever been reluctant to go to Jesus because you felt you had so far to go? When you look at the perfect, spotless life of Christ contrasted with your own sinfulness, do you become discouraged by the vastness of the gulf that separates you from Him?

Like the shackled demoniac, you know that you are firmly bound by the chains of bad habits and sins. But the Bible promises, "Draw near to God and He will draw near to you" (James 4:8).

In our story of the madman, Jesus and His disciples "sailed to the country of the Gadarenes, which is opposite Galilee" (Luke 8:26). Galilee was the center of Jesus' labors, so in going "opposite Galilee," He traveled a long way to meet the lunatic. That's a fact you don't want to miss in this story—because in it you will also see that Jesus came from His home far off in heaven to this lowly, dark world. Our planet is the antithesis of paradise.

It bears repeating: Jesus made a dangerous journey across the stormy sea to save a man completely captive to the enemy. He also crossed the ocean of space to save this one lost world. Like a shepherd searching for a lost lamb, He walked the vast cosmos to save a doomed humanity.

"Come to Me, all you who labor and are heavy laden, and I will give you rest."—Matthew 11:28

Come As You Are

During a war between France and England, a French whaling vessel set sail on an extended voyage. At some point during their long journey, the crew ran out of drinking water. Unfortunately, the only port they could reach before perishing of thirst was one controlled by England.

Of course, they were afraid to approach because they were sure the ship would be seized and they would be taken captives. Eventually, however, they raised a distress signal . . . and the answer came that they could enter in peace because the war was over. The sailors could hardly believe it; they thought for sure that it was a trick. But with death staring them in the face, they had no better option. So, they limped into the port, risking their freedom. When they docked, they found that the report was true—peace had been declared and they were in no danger.

One of the most sublime truths in the story of the demoniac is that this helpless captive of Satan came to Jesus just as he was. He could do nothing to save himself.

A pastor's work includes periodically visiting with members of the congregation. Some of these members offer all kinds of excuses as to why the pastor shouldn't visit them and their families—at least not right now. "The house is a mess!" "My hair is a mess." "I haven't had a chance to clean up and change my clothes." "I don't feel very good today." And the list goes on.

The demoniac had more reason to declare himself unprepared to meet Jesus than just about anyone else. He could easily have argued that his yard— his cemetery!—was a mess. He could have said his clothes were a mess—or more accurately, that he was naked and ashamed. He probably didn't feel very healthy either. But he understood his desperate need, so he approached Jesus just as he was. And Jesus received him despite his deplorable condition.

The world is full of people languishing somewhere on the sea of life, facing eternal death because they have no "water of life" aboard their vessel. Instead of heading their ship toward God's harbor, they reason, "God is a tyrant! We can't trust Him. No, He will destroy us."

I want to shout a message over all the waters that cover this earth: "Peace has been declared! Come into the harbor, where you will find the bread of life and living water to spare!" Scripture tells us, the Holy Spirit says, " 'Come!' . . . And let him who thirsts come. Whoever desires, let him take the water of life freely" (Revelation 22:17).

Just as I am, without one plea,
But that Thy blood was shed for me,
And that Thou bidst me come to Thee,
O Lamb of God, I come, I come.*

---

*From the hymn "Just As I Am"; words by Charlotte Elliot.

"Blessed are the poor in spirit, for theirs is the kingdom of heaven."—Matthew 5:3

Running on Empty

Dwight Moody used to tell the story of an artist in nineteenth-century England who wanted to paint a picture of the prodigal son. He searched through the madhouses, the poorhouses, and the prisons to find a man wretched enough to represent the wayward prodigal, but he couldn't find one.

Then one day the painter was walking down a street and met a beggar whom he thought would do well. He told the ragged fellow that he would pay him if he came to his home and sat for a portrait. The beggar agreed, and they chose a day for him to come.

However, when the man appeared at the artist's home, the artist didn't recognize him.

The beggar said, "You made an appointment with me for a portrait today."

The painter replied, "That's not possible; we've never met! It must have been some other artist. Indeed, I was to see a poor beggar at this very hour."

"But I am he," the man said.

"You? But what have you done with yourself?"

"Well, I thought I would dress myself up a bit before I got painted."

"I wanted you just as you were," replied the artist. "Now, you are no use to me."

Martin Luther said, "God creates from nothing, so until we become nothing, He can make nothing of us." When the demoniac went to Jesus, he went absolutely empty-handed. The only possessions he could offer Jesus were his miserable soul, imprisoned heart, deranged mind, and mangled chains. And much like the prodigal son returning home, when we go to Jesus, we go with dirty clothes, with empty hands and pockets—and an empty tank of gas.

Let me explain: I hate running out of gas. Like most people, I fill up long before the warning light starts flashing. But during my thirty years of driving, sometimes I have managed to come very close. On one occasion, I desperately searched for a gas station in a strange town, while driving as economically as I could. I accelerated slowly and coasted whenever possible. Finally, I found a service station, and I felt great relief. And just as I pulled up to the pump, my car began to sputter on its last few drops of fuel. I was totally empty when I made it to the station.

This is how we go to Jesus—sputtering and empty.

Peter, Andrew, James, and John left their nets and boats to follow Jesus. Matthew walked away from his tax booth. They gave up all they had. But when Jesus told the rich young ruler to sell everything he had and give the proceeds to the poor, he refused. "He was sad . . . and went away sorrowful, for he had great possessions" (Mark 10:22). Unwilling to lose the security of his earthly riches, he walked away from Jesus with his pockets full and his heart empty.

BROKEN CHAINS

Jesus asks each of us to cut our ties to every earthly possession before we can be His disciples. We must each place on the altar anything and everything that comes between our heart and Him. "For where your treasure is, there your heart will be also" (Matthew 6:21).

In order to save us, God may allow us to endure various trials so He can get our attention. Sometimes He must place a burden on our backs to get us to fall on our knees. This might come in the form of an illness or a family or financial crisis.

For instance, a man in his fifties who accepted Christ at one of my evangelistic meetings tells this story. He once had a good government job, a nice home, a loving family, and money in the bank. One weekend, he drove to Reno with some friends to gamble in one of the casinos. Like most people, he lost money at the poker table, the roulette wheel, and the slot machines.

Naïve to the addictive pull of fast money, he returned the next week with high hopes of winning back what he had lost. Instead, however, he lost more. He began neglecting his family and work commitments as his desire to recoup the lost money grew. But he just kept losing. By the time I met him, he was facing a $60,000 credit-card debt—even after he had mortgaged his home, emptied his bank account, and cashed in on his retirement. What's more, he was drinking heavily and had lost his job, and his wife had divorced him.

Spiritually and literally bankrupt, he came to

Jesus and found real riches. As the hymns say:

"Take my silver and my gold;
Not a mite would I withhold."*

"Nothing in my hand I bring,
Simply to the cross I cling;
Naked, come to Thee for dress;
Helpless, look to Thee for grace;
Foul, I to the fountain fly;
Wash me, Savior, or I die."†

*"Beloved, I beg you . . . abstain from fleshly lusts which
war against the soul."—1 Peter 2:11*

Two Spirits

A teenager in Virginia was shocked to find a two-headed turtle behind her home. She caught the poor creature and watched as the two freakish heads did a tug-of-war over a piece of food that she gave them—or it!

According to scientists, two-headedness can occur in all animals, but generally, such creatures don't live long. Each head tends to work independently of the other, controlling its own side of the body, and

---

*From the hymn "Take My Life and Let It Be"; words by Frances R. Havergal.

†From the hymn "Rock of Ages"; words by Augustus M. Toplady.

therefore creating disunity, confusion, and frustration. Unless one head takes primary control, the creature will soon die from starvation and indecision.

A war is raging in the heart and mind of every person on the planet—a war between the spirit and the flesh. In one sense, it is really a war between two spirits.

If you asked people, "Would you like to be Spirit possessed?" most would probably fold their arms and emphatically shake their heads. "No, thank you!" We almost always equate "possession" with evil spirits. But two contrasting spirits are seeking residence in our hearts and minds: the Spirit of God and the spirit of Satan (see 1 Corinthians 2:12). The primary motive of one of these spirits is love, and of the other, selfishness. At times, each of us feels these forces pulling us in opposite directions.

God designed our minds to be the dwelling place of the Holy Spirit. One good example of this is the prophet Daniel, who was chosen "because an excellent spirit was in him" (Daniel 6:3). It was also true of the martyr Stephen, "a man full of faith and the Holy Spirit" (Acts 6:5). And who could forget John the Baptist, "filled with the Holy Spirit, even from his mother's womb" (Luke 1:15).

For these men and for us, the most important part of the body is the two-pound electrochemical computer called the brain. Your hands and feet do the bidding of your brain, so that is the space that God's Spirit wants to inhabit. Of course, the devil is constantly probing our mental defenses for weak spots so that he can break in and take complete control of our thoughts.

However, Jesus knocks politely at the door of our hearts and minds, tenderly calling our names and gently requesting permission to enter and abide in us (see Revelation 3:20). We should open the door to Him, because He is perfectly filled with the Spirit of God. "For God does not give the Spirit by measure" (John 3:34).

Dwight Moody said, "God commands us to be filled with the Spirit, and if we are not filled, it is because we are living beneath our privileges." How can we receive this filling?

"Blessed are the pure in heart, for they shall see God."
—*Matthew 5:8*

Power in Purity

One of the knights of King Arthur's round table was Sir Galahad, who was called the "Maiden Knight" because of his pure life. He was much more noble than the well-known Sir Lancelot, who had an affair with Guinevere. Alfred Tennyson, the English poet, reports Sir Galahad as saying, "My strength is as the strength of ten, because my heart is pure."

We looked in depth at the devil's deadly devices in section two. After seeing them, you might be thinking we should live in fear of his crafty power. But the story of the demoniac's deliverance teaches the opposite. When we are abiding in Christ, we need not fear the enemy. "You are of God, little children, and have overcome them, because He who is in you is greater than he who is in the world" (1 John 4:4). We need to remember always this crucial fact: We do not become strong for God by virtue of our own right-eousness. Many professed Christians are crippled in their service because their unforsaken sins sap the vitality from their faith.

It was after the disciples had spent ten days hum-bling themselves and putting aside their differences that God poured out the power of His Spirit (Acts 1:8). "Those who wait on the Lord shall renew their strength; they shall mount up with wings like eagles, they shall run and not be weary, they shall walk and not faint" (Isaiah 40:31).

I once read about a rather rough, uncultured bach-elor who fell in love with a beautiful vase in a shop window that he passed each day as he walked to work. He eventually bought the vase and placed it on the mantelpiece by his bedroom window. It soon became a bold judgment on the state of his room— the curtains were faded and dirty, the old chair was oozing stuffing, and the wallpaper was peeling. The bachelor decided that he had to clean up the room to make it worthy of the vase. Gradually, one project at a time, the bedroom came alive. It was rejuvenated. The beauty of one special object inspired the trans-formation.

This story illustrates the transforming influence that Jesus has when we receive Him into our hearts.

Jesus will make our hearts purer, and when He does, we will become better able to resist Satan's temptations. There's power in purity.

> *"The Spirit of the Lord God is upon Me,*
> *because the Lord has anointed Me to preach*
> *good tidings to the poor; He has sent Me to heal*
> *the brokenhearted, to proclaim liberty to the captives,*
> *and the opening of the prison to those who*
> *are bound."—Isaiah 61:1*

Delivering the Captives

A miner approached the famous preacher G. Campbell Morgan and said he'd do anything to believe that God would forgive him of all his sins. "But," the miner lamented, "I cannot believe He will if I just turn to Him. It is too cheap."

Dr. Morgan responded with a question. "You were working in the mine today. How did you get out of the pit?"

He answered, "The way I usually do. I got into the elevator cage and was pulled to the top."

"How much did you pay to come out of the pit?" the pastor asked.

"I didn't pay anything."

Morgan said, "Weren't you afraid to trust yourself to that cage? Was it not too cheap?"

The man replied, "Oh, no! It was cheap for me, but it cost the company a lot of money." Suddenly the miner saw the light! While our salvation comes to us freely by faith and not by anything that we do, Jesus paid an immense price for it. The gift that is free to us cost God a great deal.

The most eloquent plea that the demoniac could offer was his own desperate helplessness. But he came anyway, and Jesus heard the prayer of his heart. "The Spirit also helps in our weaknesses. For we do not know what we should pray for as we ought, but the Spirit Himself makes intercession for us with groanings which cannot be uttered" (Romans 8:26).

All it took was one word from Jesus—"Go!"—and the man was free.

While the demoniac had once been a slave to demon possession, he was now free. While he was once wild and uncontrollable, he now sat quietly at Jesus' feet. While once he was an instrument of Satan, he was now a witness to Christ's power. Once naked, he was now clothed. Once a menace to society, he was now a messenger with words of deliverance and healing.

A young girl watched a plane write an advertisement against the blue backdrop of the sky. She became a little puzzled when the words began to disappear. Then suddenly she piped up. "Maybe Jesus has an eraser!" she said.

In a sense, she was right. Just as skywriting disappears, Jesus wipes away all things for which we have repented. No matter how much we mature as Christians and try desperately to compensate for our past misdeeds, memories of these failures can rise up and haunt us. But with God's forgiveness, they will fade away.

Jesus does have an eraser.

"Jesus said to him, 'If you can believe, all things are possible to him who believes.' "—Mark 9:23

The Power of Faith

A friend gave me a racquet worth two hundred dollars when he heard how much I like playing racquetball. (I think he had purchased it at 75 percent off.) I looked forward to trying this ultralight, powerful racquet. In fact, I thought to myself, "Now I'm going to win for a change, because I've got this expensive, high-tech racquet."

Sure enough, the next time we played, I won all three games. Afterward, as I was putting my racquet away, I discovered that I had been playing with my old racquet. Evidently, I had pulled the old racquet out of my bag instead of the new one without noticing what I was doing. And since I thought I was playing with a two-hundred-dollar racquet, I played much better—though the entire time I really was using the same old, crooked thirty-nine-dollar racquet I'd had all along!

Faith is powerful! Aware of this truth, major corporations pay motivational speakers thousands of dollars a day to inspire their sales employees. These speakers say that when people truly believe in something, they have the "power of positive thinking," which can influence them to do extraordinary things.

Even the twelve-step addiction-recovery programs incorporate faith as one of the major keys to success. Step 8 says: "I not only believe, but 'act as if' my higher power is guiding my life and situations. My life is one of simple reliance on my Higher Power."

The Bible also promises great things for those who have faith. From the Old Testament to the New, it has always been about having faith. Habakkuk 2:4 tells us, "The just shall live by his faith." And in the New Testament, Paul wrote, "By grace you have been saved through faith" (Ephesians 2:8).

After the disciples tried and failed to cast a demon out of a boy, they called on Jesus, who rebuked the demon and cured the child almost instantly. The disciples asked Jesus, " 'Why could we not cast it out?' " Jesus answered, " 'Because of your unbelief; for assuredly, I say to you, if you have faith as a mustard seed, you will say to this mountain, "Move from here to there," and it will move; and nothing will be impossible for you' " (Matthew 17:18-20). And when Jesus faced the demoniac, He believed He had the power to set the poor soul free.

"Without faith it is impossible to please Him, for he who comes to God must believe that He is, and that He is a rewarder of those who diligently seek Him" (Hebrews 11:6). We won't be able to break any of the chains that bind us if we don't have faith.

Ask Christ to increase your faith today so that He can do even greater things in your life. If your faith is fragile, you can even pray like the father of the demon-possessed boy, "Lord, I believe; help my unbelief!" (Mark 9:24).

"Looking unto Jesus, the author and finisher of our faith."—Hebrews 12:2

We Are Changed by Beholding

A godly pastor was approached by a member of his congregation—a physician who was concerned about the pastor's busy schedule. Handing the minister some theater tickets, he said, "You work too hard! You need some recreation, so go to this movie and have a good time."

His pastor looked at the tickets, knowing he could not conscientiously attend. He replied kindly, "Thank you, but I can't take them. I can't go."

"Why not?" asked the physician.

"Doctor, it's this way," he answered. "You're a surgeon, and when you operate, you scrub your hands meticulously until you are especially clean. You wouldn't dare operate with dirty hands. Likewise, I'm a servant of Christ. I deal with precious human souls. I wouldn't dare do my service with a dirty heart."

Probably the most lethal influences eroding the purity of modern Christians are the TV and VCR/DVD. Many professed Christians who would never be found guilty of engaging in the actual deeds of murder, adultery, robbery, and lying still participate vicariously in these sins every week by willingly beholding them on television programs and through videos.

King David promised, "I will set nothing wicked before my eyes" (Psalm 101:3). Not only does Scripture condemn those acts, but judgment is pronounced against those who "have pleasure in them that do them" (Romans 1:32, KJV). In others words, those who revel in watching others commit these sins are committing them in their hearts.

There is a dainty butterfly with a wingspread of less than an inch. It's beautiful—bright blue wings with jewel-like gold spots. But as lovely as it is to behold, it has a disgusting diet. Instead of floating from flower to flower and feeding on nectar, it descends to earth and feeds on dung.

Millions of professed Christians act like these butterflies. They go to church, but they feed on filth at home as they watch TV programs and videos that profane God's name and depict violations of every commandment. If we ever hope to be pure in heart, we must guard the avenues to our souls. What we choose to watch, read, and hear should measure up to the standard of Christ's approval.

> I beseech you therefore, brethren, by the mercies of God, that you present your bodies a living sacrifice, holy, acceptable to God, which is

your reasonable service. And do not be conformed to this world, but be transformed by the
renewing of your mind, that you may prove
what is that good and acceptable and perfect will
of God (Romans 12:1, 2).

The demoniac's deliverance is beautiful to consider. As this poor, raging soul stood before the
Savior and beheld Him, he was transformed into
the image of his new Master. Scripture often testi-
fies to the principle that we become like the person or thing we worship. "We all, with unveiled
face, beholding as in a mirror the glory of the Lord,
are being transformed into the same image from
glory to glory, just as by the Spirit of the Lord"
(2 Corinthians 3:18).

So, as we turn our eyes upon Jesus and gaze every day at His pure and spotless life, we find ourselves longing for that same purity. But if we fill
our minds with the wicked and frivolous material
that is so prevalent in movies, magazines, and on
television, we will find that carnal cravings constantly pollute our heart. They will sear our conscience, and we will lose our hunger and thirst for
righteousness.

It is worthy to note that the animal-like demoniac
lived in a region peppered with idols. Many were of
gods that were part animal and part man. Surrounded by these animalistic images, the madman
became like the idols he beheld. The Bible says this
will happen to anyone who falls into the same trap.

"Those who make them are like them; so is everyone who trusts in them" (Psalm 135:18).

Those who worship and follow Jesus are gradually transformed into His likeness. That's what makes them *Christian,* "followers of Christ." Scripture notes this transformation in Jesus' disciples: "When they saw the boldness of Peter and John, and perceived that they were uneducated and untrained men, they marveled. And they realized that they had been with Jesus" (Acts 4:13).

"When he saw Jesus, he cried out, and fell down before Him."—Luke 8:28

Admitting Our Guilt

The czar of Russia visited a prison in Moscow one day. While he was surveying a jail cell full of criminals, the inmates crowded against the bars and began to beg him for freedom. In one form or another, they all pled that they were innocent and had been falsely accused.

The czar noticed one man sitting quietly alone on a bench in the back of the cell. The czar summoned the man and asked him, "Why are you here?"

The criminal responded, "I am a thief, your Highness. I am guilty of stealing a wagon."

The czar ordered the guards to release this man, commenting, "I do not want an admitted thief to contaminate all these innocent men."

Honest, heartfelt repentance is a prerequisite to our being cleansed. Before we can be transformed, we must "come clean" through confession of our sins.

Even before that, we must have a real desire to be free from sin. True repentance means not only that we are sorry for our sins but also that we're sorry enough to stop doing them. Some act like confessing sins once a week at church gives people a clean slate to fill up again. That's not true repentance!

The Bible talks about two kinds of repentance. Judas repented and then hung himself. Peter repented and wept bitterly, and he was converted. He changed! God wants us to be sorry for our sins—sorry enough to change, sorry enough to stop doing them. "Whoever confesses *and forsakes them [sins],* will have mercy" (Proverbs 28:13, emphasis added).

Why does God want us to confess our sins?

When I was a new Christian, I would say, "God, we need to have a talk. You better sit down and brace yourself; there are some things I have to tell you"—as though in confessing, I was telling Him something He didn't know. But God already knows everything! So, we might ask, "If God knows everything, why pray?" Jesus tells us that He knows the things we need before we pray (Matthew 6:8), but He still tells us to ask. In the same way, He knows our sins before we confess but still asks us to confess them.

God asks us to confess for at least a couple reasons. First, it is simply polite. When we hurt a person, we should say we're sorry. Every time we sin, we hurt ourselves, we hurt others, and we hurt God. So when we confess, we say to God, "I'm sorry." It's only proper to apologize.

Second, it's God's method for removing the feelings of guilt from our lives. It helps us to believe we are truly forgiven. I think some people have never felt the freedom and peace that God wants us to enjoy as Christians because their confession is so shallow and brief. In many cases, we spend twenty, thirty, and even forty years sinning daily, hourly, offending our heavenly Father—only to find a passing moment in which to say flippantly, "Lord, forgive my sins." No one will find solace and relief in that kind of shallow, shabby confession.

Now, I'm not saying that we should specifically confess every sin that we've ever committed. Nobody can remember all the wrong things he or she has done. However, we should try to be as specific as possible.

How specific can we be when some of us can't remember even what we've done in one day?

Here's something I think works very well. I don't remember every lie that I've ever told, but I knew I was a liar. I don't remember everything I've stolen, but I knew I was a thief. So when it came time for me to repent of those sins, I took a piece of paper and wrote down, "I'm a thief. I'm a liar." If you do remember something specific, it might be the Holy

Spirit placing it on your heart. If you're afraid of forgetting something, don't be. If you ask God to help you, the Holy Spirit will bring to your remembrance the sins you need to confess. You might have a long list by now!*

When you've compiled your list, kneel down and say, "Father, I am confessing my sins. I am guilty of these things." Then read your list to God. I know it might be painful, but trust me, it's extremely healthy for your soul! Finish your prayer by saying, "Please forgive me, for Christ's sake."†

We have the promise, "If we confess our sins, He is faithful and just to forgive us our sins," and He will also "cleanse us from all unrighteousness" (1 John 1:9). That means freedom not only from the penalty of sin, which is death, but from the power of sin. When you confess like this, God will give you power to do right and to make changes in your life. "If anyone is in Christ, he is a new creation; old things

---

*One of the other advantages of this kind of detailed confession is that you are admitting that your sins are sins. In other words, it's easy enough to say, "Lord, I'm a sinner," but when you finally say, "Lord, I'm a gossip," it could be the first time you have specifically acknowledged gossip as a sin. This allows the Holy Spirit even more opportunity to change that failing of yours.

†We must also not neglect confessing to other people whom we've offended. For instance, if you've stolen something, you should tell the person you've wronged and then, as far as possible, try to repay that person (see Ezekiel 33:15). If you've hurt someone, you need to tell them that you're sorry and try to reconcile the relationship.

have passed away; behold, all things have become new" (2 Corinthians 5:17).*

*"Then the demons . . . entered the swine,
and the herd ran violently down the steep place
into the lake and drowned."—Luke 8:33*

Possessed Pigs and Sinking Swine

Someone once observed about the swine in the demoniac's story, "Had our Lord achieved such a miracle today, He would have been in deep trouble. Next, the EPA would have been investigating the pollution of the lake because of the disposal of pig carcasses. Then PETA would have been up in arms over such outrageous cruelty to animals. Then, pork brokers would have been greatly distressed over the sudden increase in pork prices because of the shortage of hogs."

This deadly miracle seems out of character for Jesus, who we typically see healing people and saving lives. The only other time a command of His resulted in death was when He cursed the fig tree. Why did Christ allow the demons to destroy the swine?

In part, Jesus let the demons enter the swine because He considered it appropriate to pair unclean things with other unclean things. The Bible classi-

---

*After you've confessed your sins, take the list and set it on fire, or tie it to a rock and throw it in the ocean (see Micah 7:19).

fies swine as among the most unclean creatures. "Their flesh you shall not eat, and their carcasses you shall not touch. They are unclean to you" (Leviticus11:8). Pigs and devils go together like skunks and stink.*

Pigs are a symbol of the lost who reject salvation. "Do not give what is holy to the dogs; nor cast your pearls before swine, lest they trample them under their feet, and turn and tear you in pieces" (Matthew 7:6). Ultimately, all the demons and the people who follow them will be thrown into a lake of fire and brimstone (Revelation 20:10, 15)—a consequence of their own making. According to the proverb, "A dog returns to his own vomit [and] a sow, having washed, to her wallowing in the mire" (2 Peter 2:22).

But Jesus also had a positive reason to allow this cholesterol catastrophe. What the devil thought would be the undoing of Jesus' work in the area actually served to magnify the miracle of salvation. All three synoptic Gospels mention this story of the drowning pigs, evidencing how far the story of the madman spread. The devil's attempts to stop God's work often backfire and become the greatest evidence for His miracles.

We see this truth in other biblical stories: the bodies of the Egyptian soldiers that floated onto the

---

*In the parable of the prodigal son, Jesus describes the wayward boy as feeding pigs—meaning he had reached the very bottom of a sinful life and was forced to work at the very bottom of society. This picture greatly disturbed the listening Jews.

shores of the Red Sea confirmed the miracle of the final Exodus victory. The scorched bodies of the soldiers who threw Shadrach, Meshach, and Abednego into the furnace confirmed the miracle of their survival. The pile of bones at the bottom of the lion's den reinforced the miracle of Daniel's deliverance from the great cats. And the Roman soldiers guarding the tomb of Jesus became the first and most compelling witnesses of His resurrection.

Thus, when two thousand bloated carcasses of pigs began to wash up on shores all around the sea of Galilee, the story of this miraculous deliverance of the demoniac was multiplied many times over—proving the miracle to everyone living in the region. "We know that all things work together for good to those who love God" (Romans 8:28).

*I*n the previous pages of this section, we've seen the importance of coming to Jesus just as we are. The biblical term for this first step of salvation is justification. This means that when we first come to Jesus, He accepts us, forgives us, and looks upon us as if we had never sinned.

In the next few pages, we'll shift our focus to the next step of salvation, sanctification. How do we stay with Jesus once we've come to Him? How do we live holy lives that are consistent with our Christian commitment? Knowing how to avoid and resist temptation is a very important component in this experience.

Part 2: Living Like Jesus

"Finally, my brethren, be strong in the Lord and in the power of His might. Put on the whole armor of God, that you may be able to stand against the wiles of the devil. For we do not wrestle against flesh and blood, but against principalities, against powers, against the rulers of the darkness of this age, against spiritual hosts of wickedness in the heavenly places."—Ephesians 6:10-12

Breaking the Chains of Temptation

One day, a young skylark discovered a fox that would trade him worms for his feathers. The deal was one feather for two worms. The next day, as the young skylark was flying high in the sky with his very wise father, his father said, "You know, son, we skylarks should be the happiest of all birds. See our brave wings! They lift us high in the air, nearer and nearer to God."

But the young bird didn't hear him; all he saw was an old fox with worms. So down he flew, plucked two feathers from his wings, and had a feast of worms. This went on day after day, until eventually autumn came and it was time to fly south. But the young skylark couldn't fly anymore, having exchanged the power of flight for worms. The next time the skylark was seen, he was hopping through the snow, trying to outrun a fox.

We're constantly tempted to exchange our wings for worms. The Bible warns us to flee temptation (see 1 Timothy 6:11), but many of us only crawl away, hoping it will catch up with us. Worse, sometimes temptation comes through a door that we've deliberately left open.

Suppose that you accidentally spilled gasoline all over your clothes, and somebody nearby lit a match. Where would you go? As far and as fast as you could possibly go in the opposite direction! That should be a Christian's attitude toward temptation. Paul said, "Flee fornication" and "flee from idolatry" (1 Corinthians 6:18; 10:14, KJV). It's good advice: Flee from sin, and don't leave a forwarding address.

Aurelius Augustine observed, "The devil is like a mad dog that is chained up. He is powerless to harm us when we are outside his reach. But once we enter his circle, we expose ourselves again to injury or harm."

So don't miss this: When you run from temptation, head toward God. When you do, the devil runs from you (James 4:7). "Draw nigh to God, and he will draw nigh to you" (James 4:8, KJV). When you know something is sinful, don't banter with the devil, because he is the master of rationalization—that's how Eve fell!

It breaks my heart when Christians try to justify their sins. There is no limit to the arguments with which the devil can supply you. As soon as you know something is wrong, flee! The brave run from temptation; fools flirt with it. Joseph fled when tempted by his master's wife, and he became ruler of Egypt. If we would live and reign with Christ, we also must learn to flee from temptation. Dwight Moody opined, "Excuses are the cradle . . . that Satan rocks men off to sleep in."

All temptation can be categorized into three main areas: "All that is in the world—the lust of the flesh, and the lust of the eyes, and the pride of life, is not of the Father but is of the world" (1 John 2:16). The sins classified as the lust of the flesh, the lust of the eyes, and the pride of life are all the same classes of sin that took Adam and Eve when they fell in the Garden of Eden. "So when *the woman saw* that the tree was good for food, that it was *pleasant to the eyes*, and *a tree desirable to make one wise*, she took of its fruit and ate" (Genesis 3:6, emphasis supplied).

Jesus successfully faced these same three categories of temptation in the wilderness. The power that humans lost in the Garden is the power that Jesus found in the desert.

"The way of the lazy man is like a hedge of thorns."
—Proverbs 15:19
"Do not be overcome by evil, but overcome evil with good."—Romans 12:21

Stay Busy Serving
An Italian proverb warns, "He that labors is tempted by one devil; he that is idle, by a thousand." Many people hate to be idle. That's because God created us for activity. You've heard the expression "idleness is the devil's workshop." That's not a direct Bible quote, but Ezekiel 16:49, 50 comes close: "Behold, this was the iniquity of thy sister Sodom, pride, fullness of bread, and abundance of idleness was in her and in her daughters. . . . Therefore I took them away as I saw good" (KJV).

The sin of Sodom and Gomorrah wasn't simply perversion and sexual immorality. The valley of Sodom was lush with vegetation and abundant with food. Life was easy for the inhabitants. Lot moved there because it offered him a life of leisure. But when a person doesn't have anything to do, chances are the devil will help the carnal heart concoct something evil. An idle person tempts the devil to tempt him. "See then that you walk circumspectly, not as fools but as wise, redeeming the time, because the days are evil" (Ephesians 5:15, 16).

Sin begins in the human mind, which is designed to concentrate mainly on one thing at a time. If we stay busy—especially focused on doing something good, like witnessing or helping the poor—we don't have time to think about evil. A wise spiritual advisor once noted that the best way to gain strength to resist evil is through aggressive service to others. One of the ways to stay out of trouble is to be aggressively involved in serving Jesus. When, after the Fall, God told Adam, "In the sweat of your face you shall eat bread," He intended that "curse" to be a blessing, by keeping people busy and so keeping them out of trouble (Genesis 3:19).

We also sometimes leave ourselves wide open to compromise when we don't fill the vacuum left by evicted demons and forsaken bad habits. I have known people to gain victory over one addiction only to replace it with another because they didn't find a positive substitute. Jesus warned about this:

> When an unclean spirit goes out of a man, he goes through dry places, seeking rest; and finding none, he says, "I will return to my house from which I came." And when he comes, he finds it swept and put in order. Then he goes and takes with him seven other spirits more wicked than himself, and they enter and dwell there; and the last state of that man is worse than the first (Luke 11:24-26).

If you are struggling with an eating disorder or food addiction, you can't simply give up eating. The secret is to learn to "eat what is good" (Isaiah 55:2). If you have a problem nibbling chocolate throughout the day, buy some grapes or almonds. Have you thrown away those cigarettes? Get a box of toothpicks or some sunflower seeds—but not chocolates! "Overcome evil with good" (Romans 12:21)!

If someone has insulted or cruelly used you, do not retaliate with evil, but respond with kindness. When a hawk is attacked by kingbirds, it doesn't counterattack. Instead, it soars higher and higher in ever-widening circles until the tormentors leave it alone. "If your enemy is hungry, feed him; if he is thirsty, give him a drink" (Romans 12:20). Stay active doing good, because although a good opportunity might knock only once, temptation constantly bangs on your front door.

"Examine yourselves as to whether you are in the faith. Test yourselves."—2 Corinthians 13:5
"Your body is the temple of the Holy Spirit . . . and . . . not your own."—1 Corinthians 6:19

Know and Take Care of Yourself
A Spanish proverb instructs, "Be not a baker if your head be of butter." When people join Alcoholics Anonymous, they are first supposed to admit to being alcoholics. This admission can represent a tre-

mendous breakthrough, because to do so they must recognize their weakness. Likewise, one of the first steps to becoming Christians is admitting that we are "sin-aholics."

"Therefore let him who thinks he stands take heed lest he fall" (1 Corinthians 10:12). The Bible says that we must not trust in our own strength. We must be very cautious when we begin to think we have a handle on a certain temptation and say, "It won't bother me anymore. I've got the victory!" That's when we are especially liable to falling. Some Christians are even proud they have overcome, but they're only setting themselves up for the devil to knock down. On the night Jesus was betrayed, He warned Peter, "This night, before the rooster crows twice, you will deny Me three times" (Mark 14:30). Jesus was warning Peter that he didn't know how weak he was.

This danger extends beyond the person with the weakness to those attempting to help them. When rescuers are pulling a person from rushing water, they have to be careful that they don't get pulled in too. We must always be vigilant to recognize our weakness. "Brethren, if a man be overtaken in a fault, ye which are spiritual, restore such an one in the spirit of meekness; considering thyself, lest thou also be tempted" (Galatians 6:1, KJV).

You'll also feel more confident to resist sin if you are caring for your body and mind. Temptation often comes not at our strongest moments, but during our weakest. When we are at the limits of our strength, patience, love, and health, we are tempted to be unchristian. Beware: Jesus' temptations began after forty days of fasting. He was tired and hungry. Peter was also tired, having stayed up through the night, when he denied Jesus.

Everything from lack of exercise to unbalanced body hormones might influence our ability to resist basic temptations. When we are sick or our reserves are drained, we react in negative ways. Most marital arguments occur at the end of the day when one or both spouses are tired and hungry. Get enough sleep and eat good food at regular times. One of my favorite authors also advises, "By the indulgence of perverted appetite, man loses his power to resist temptation." Excessive sweets can give you a temporary rush, only to be followed by feelings of depression and irritability.

In the same way, it's a big mistake to think that we can go up against the devil in times of temptation without first storing the ammunition of God's Word in our mind. Jesus met every temptation foisted upon Him with the words "It is written" (see, e.g., Matthew 4:4, 7, 10).

Jesus took care of His mind by knowing His Father's Word. If you expect to overcome the devil in the battles of life, you need to fortify your mind with God's truth. King David said, "Your Word I have hidden in my heart, that I might not sin against You" (Psalm 119:11).

When soldiers know they are passing through a minefield, they are very careful where they step. You might not always be able to avoid fatigue or hunger, but you can avoid sensitive discussions or demanding tasks during these volatile times. Jesus said, "The spirit indeed is willing, but the flesh is weak" (Matthew 26:41). This doesn't mean we shouldn't try to do everything in our power to improve our health and thereby our moral resolve. A good night's rest, a little exercise, and a nutritious breakfast can make us feel like we're ready to take on Goliath.

"By wise counsel you will wage your own war; . . . in a multitude of counselors there is safety."
—Proverbs 24:6
"The disciples took him by night and let him down through the wall in a large basket."—Acts 9:25

Always Have a Plan

We often stumble into sin because when we see temptation coming, we wait to see what might happen when it arrives. It's better to be prepared. Proverbs 22:3 advises, "A prudent man foresees evil and hides himself, but the simple pass on and are punished."

A wise man surveys the road for potential trouble. If he spots a band of robbers, he thinks, "I'd better hide or change routes, because I don't want to be robbed!" But the fool says, "Wow. I think there are bandits down the road. I wonder what's going to happen when they get here."

Christians often do the latter with temptation. We say, "I wonder if I'll be tempted if I watch this program, read this magazine, or drink this stuff." But Jesus said, "If thy right eye offend thee, pluck it out, and cast it from thee: for it is profitable . . . that one of thy members should perish, and not that thy whole body should be cast into hell" (Matthew 5:29, KJV).

If there's a particular temptation that you know will drag you down, take whatever measures of prevention you can, no matter how desperate, to keep from being overcome. For instance, if you want to quit smoking, avoid friends who smoke or places where you are more prone to be tempted. In the very least, plot a way of escape! If your temptation is overeating, decide to place an appropriate amount of food on your plate and to stop eating when it's gone. Millions nibble their way into sin because they don't think ahead.

Of course, one of the best possible measures against sinning is knowing where to run when it gets too hot to handle. When I board a plane, I make a mental note of the location of the emergency exits. I'm not paranoid, just prudent. For me, the very best means for overcoming temptation is recognizing that God has provided a way of escape for every one of us. Remember this passage: "No temptation has overtaken you except such as is common to man; but God is faithful, who will not allow you to be tempted beyond what you are able, but with the temptation will also make the way of escape, that you may be able to bear it" (1 Corinthians 10:13).

That's some very good news. We don't have to rely on our shaky faith; we can rely on God because He is faithful! So, when you're tempted, you can say, "God is measuring what He allows the devil to bring against me, and I'm able to handle it by His grace." You never have to say, "I can't bear to resist the devil any longer." By saying that, you'd be calling God a liar!

When the children of Israel were leaving Egypt, they found themselves trapped. The Egyptian army was chasing them, and there were mountains on both sides of them and a sea in front. It seemed like a hopeless situation. But God had promised that He would be faithful, and He provided a way of escape.

The Bible is full of stories like this, in which the situation seemed hopeless but God proved to be faithful. When it looked like there was no food to feed the crowd following Jesus, God multiplied the loaves and fishes to satisfy them—just as He had fed Elijah and the Israelites. He'll use dramatic rescue attempts to help you too. Even with the most devilish temptation at your doorstep, remember these stories and make up your mind to trust God and watch for His way of escape.

"A righteous man may fall seven times and rise again."—Proverbs 24:16

Surviving a Fall

Here's a powerful message from the Reformer John Knox:

Mark what has been the practice of the Devil from the beginning, most cruelly to rage against God's children, when God begins to show them his mercy. And therefore marvel not, dearly beloved, though this should happen to you. If Satan fume and roar against you, whether it be against your bodies by persecution, or inwardly in your consciences by a spiritual battle, do not be discouraged, as though you were less acceptable in God's presence, or that Satan might at any time prevail against you. No! . . . I have good hope, and my prayer will likewise be, that you may be so strengthened, that the world and Satan himself may understand and perceive, that God is fighting your battle.

One of the most important keys to overcoming temptation is the knowledge that if you are in Christ, you have great power to resist wrong (Jude 24). To abide in Him is to abide in His Spirit. And Galatians 5:16 says, "Walk in the Spirit, and you shall not fulfill the lust of the flesh."

Noah, Enoch, and Abraham walked with God. We can do the same today by getting on our knees to petition for strength. Rather than let us fall when we're trustingly pleading for His help, God will send every angel in heaven to save us from sin. God has made us free moral agents, and the devil cannot make us sin. But we must choose to follow Jesus rather than the lies of the devil. So by God's grace, you and I can resist every temptation.

However, remember that you needn't give up if you do fall. A Chinese proverb says, "You don't drown by falling in the water. You drown by staying there." Many people who fall down, stay down. They say, "Oh, well, I'm lost now—I may as well surrender to every other temptation." God can help you recover lost territory, and He will save you from future temptations.

The devil may dishearten you with his wicked whisperings, "I know you! I tempted you, and you did it! You're no good. You call yourself a Christian, but you're just a hypocrite. In fact, you aren't even saved!"

I believe the Christian life is progressive. The Bible promises, "My little children, these things write I to you, so that you may not sin. And if anyone sins, we have an Advocate with the Father, Jesus Christ the righteous" (1 John 2:1). If you sin—and we all do—don't give up. If the devil tricks you, and you fall down, don't stay down. Don't let your past failures be an excuse for future compromise. God can help you overcome everything. You take it just one day and one step at a time.

Of course, the most powerful motive for resisting any temptation is your love for God. You know that sin hurts God, so, when you're tempted, you need to say out loud, "I can't do that because I love God."

Erwin W. Lutzer said, "Our response to temptation is an accurate barometer of our love for God." The more you love Jesus, the less the attractions of the devil will hold sway over you. Remember how much Jesus loves you by remembering the cross when you are tempted, and then return that love by resisting the evil before you.

We're all tempted, but the Lord has promised that we can be overcomers through the "exceeding great and precious promises" found in the Scriptures. Jesus will teach us how to overcome. The devil could not make Jesus sin, nor can he make us sin. Give thanks to God, "who gives us the victory through our Lord Jesus Christ" (1 Corinthians 15:57). Ask Him for overcoming power, and joyfully dive into the pages of His Word.

"They . . . found the man from whom the demons had departed, sitting at the feet of Jesus."—Luke 8:35

Sitting at His Feet

Sitting at someone's feet is a posture of submission. This position also represents a willingness to learn. While the demoniac sat at Jesus' feet, I'm certain that Jesus was teaching him how to avoid the mistakes that had led to his deplorable state.

Mary Magdalene, out of whom Jesus cast seven devils, also recognized her need to spend regular time sitting at Jesus' feet to avoid the gauntlet of temptations that plague every human soul. It's a great story!

He [Jesus] entered a certain village; and a certain woman named Martha welcomed Him into her house. And she had a sister called Mary, who also sat at Jesus' feet and heard His word. But Martha was distracted with much serving, and she approached Him and said, "Lord, do You not care that my sister has left me to serve alone? Therefore tell her to help me." And Jesus answered and said to her, "Martha, Martha, you are worried and troubled about many things. But one thing is needed, and Mary has chosen that good part, which will not be taken away from her" (Luke 10:38-42).

I could hear Brother Harold's oversized, three-wheel cycle squeak up behind me as I walked down the street. Brother Harold was a living legend among the young people in Palm Springs. He was a seventy-year-old saint; a Jewish Christian, who knew how to "walk the walk" and "talk the talk."

Brother Harold's day began at four o'clock in the morning with two hours of Bible study and prayer, followed by a few hours on the street handing out tracts. Next he was off to the hospital. As a self-appointed chaplain, he would visit the rooms and share with the patients an encouraging scripture or two—all from memory. I will never forget how his voice trembled with reverence when he quoted the Bible. One time at an early-morning prayer meeting, I thought I saw his old, bearded face shine as he prayed.

BROKEN CHAINS

I was a new Christian at the time, still struggling to separate my former hippie philosophy from the truths of the Bible. Frequently confused, I was feeling a bit like a failure as a Christian. Brother Harold always had a way of knowing who needed encouragement.

"What a glorious day God has given us!" he called as he pulled up beside me. He was always so "up."

"Yeah, nice day," I responded. I must not have been very convincing, because he studied me for a moment with a loving yet concerned expression.

"How long can you hold your breath, Doug?" Brother Harold finally asked with a twinkle in his eye. His question surprised me, but I seldom missed an opportunity to brag. In school, I had played a little game of seeing how long I could hold my breath while waiting for the class bell to ring. So I boasted, "I can hold my breath for four minutes, if I hyperventilate first."

"Then you should not go any longer than that without praying," he said. "God's Word tells us, 'Pray without ceasing.' "

Next he asked, "How often do you eat?"

I was already beginning to sense where he was leading. "About two or three times a day," I said hesitantly.

"Well, that's how often you should read or meditate on God's Word." Then he added, "Doug, what will happen to your body if you never exercise it?"

"I suppose I'll get weak and flabby," I responded.

"That's right," said Brother Harold, "and that is what will happen to your faith if you don't use it and share it."

As he pedaled away, Brother Harold called over his shoulder, "The same laws that apply to your physical body also apply to your spiritual health." That day thirty years ago in Palm Springs, Brother Harold directed me to the secret weapon for the Christian. That weapon is our personal devotions—Bible study, prayer, and witnessing. The practice of having personal devotions is not a secret weapon because anyone has tried to keep it hidden. Rather, it's unknown because so many people have neglected it. We need to spend time at Jesus' feet.

We've talked about preparing ourselves to avoid temptation when it comes, and we've learned that we'll want to be prepared to meet the temptations that we'll face only when we truly love God. To love God, we must to get to know Him. We'll explore this a little more in the next few pages.

"He healed many who were sick
with various diseases, and cast out many demons;
and He did not allow the demons to speak,
because they knew Him."—Mark 1:34

Knowing the Lord

In a 1983 Gallup poll, Americans were asked, "Who do you think Jesus is?" About 70 percent of those interviewed said Jesus was not just another man. Forty-two percent answered that He was God among men. Twenty-seven percent felt Jesus was only human, but divinely called. Another 9 percent believed Jesus was divine because He embodied the best of humanity. Yet 81 percent of Americans considered themselves to be Christians.

Many of those 81 percent in the poll might be like the people Jesus was talking about when He said, "Many will say to Me in that day, 'Lord, Lord, have we not prophesied in Your name, cast out demons in Your name, and done many wonders in Your name?' And then I will declare to them, 'I never knew you; depart from Me, you who practice lawlessness!' " (Matthew 7:22, 23). They are lost despite their beliefs.

The Bible clearly indicates that we gain salvation not by doing good works but from something much different. The Lord warned that many would make the fatal mistake of thinking that good works guarantee salvation. It's hard to believe that it is even possible to do good works for Jesus without having a saving relationship with Him. In fact, what Paul wrote to Titus seems applicable to those people who have no relationship with the Lord: "They profess to know God, but in works they deny Him, being abominable, disobedient, and disqualified for every good work" (Titus 1:16).

Although the Bible is clear that we are not saved by works, it also clearly says that we will be condemned or rewarded based on what we've done:

"The dead were judged according to their works, by the things which were written in the books" (Revelation 20:12). "Behold, I am coming quickly, and My reward is with Me, to give to every one according to his work" (Revelation 22:12).

In the judgment, many will claim to know God, but their works will reveal a different story. The key then is that once we really know God, the genuine good works for which we will be rewarded will follow. But how do we get to know Him? How do we sit at Jesus' feet like the demoniac and Mary while He is in heaven?

George Mueller said this about God's Book: "The vigor of our spiritual life will be in exact proportion to the place held by the Bible in our life and thoughts." John 17:3 affirms, " 'This is eternal life, that they may know You, the only true God, and Jesus Christ whom You have sent' " (John 17:3). This knowledge that saves is not a casual understanding of biblical doctrine. The devil understands, but that will not save him. James 2:19, KJV, says, "The devils also believe, and tremble."*

So, to know God in this way must mean to have a loving relationship with Him. " 'I will betroth

---

*Still, it's amazing to consider that the demons always seemed to recognize Jesus. Those that possessed the demoniac certainly did. The demons that possessed him "cried out with a loud voice and said, 'What have I to do with You, Jesus, Son of the Most High God?' " (Mark 5:7). Unfortunately, as we've already seen, many of Jesus' own people don't know Him that well.

you to me in faithfulness, and you shall know the LORD' " (Hosea 2:20). We can't really obey the Lord unless we love Him first, which is why Jesus said, "If you love Me, keep My commandments" (John 14:15).*

It's the same with having faith—where do we get it? Paul tells us, "So then faith comes by hearing, and hearing by the word of God" (Romans 10:17).

The formula that changes lives is very simple: To obey God, we must love Him. To love God, we must know Him. And to know Him, we must spend regular time with Him, at His feet, learning who He really is. It's true with any relationships—to know or trust people, we must first take time to communicate with them. They talk to us, and we to them.

God speaks to us through His Word, and we speak to Him through prayer. The better we know God, the more we will love Him. The more we love Him, the better we will serve Him. Genuine service for God can spring only from a genuine knowledge of Him. " 'By their fruits you will know them' " (Matthew 7:20).

A prominent prince chose to be present at the execution of a noted criminal. He was deeply moved as he observed the distress that he saw in the face

---

*A little later, Jesus said, " 'He who has My commandments and keeps them, it is he who loves Me' " (John 14:21). Jesus' repetition of this thought about keeping the commandments suggests He considered it very important. (See also 1 John 2:4.)

of the condemned man and was moved to ask: "Is there any request that you wish to make before you die?"

The man answered, "Yes, please. I would like to have a drink of water."

The water was provided, but the criminal was trembling so badly that he found it very difficult to bring the cup to his lips. On seeing this, the prince said to him, "Do not fear; take your time. Your life will be spared until you drink that water."

At that, the prisoner paused, dashed the water to the ground, and then turned to the prince and said with great confidence, "I take you at your word."

The prince was not displeased, nor was he made angry at the man's presumption. He commanded the prisoner to be released, pleased that even this unworthy and undeserving man should have so much confidence in the authority of his word.

We cannot overstress the importance of simple belief in the promise of God that His Word saves us. It is our privilege to take advantage of His great mercy. Scripture tells us that God has "given to us exceedingly great and precious promises, that through these you may be partakers of the divine nature, having escaped the corruption that is in the world through lust" (2 Peter 1:4).

"In the morning, having risen a long while before daylight, He [Jesus] went out and departed to a solitary place; and there He prayed."—Mark 1:35

Fresh Bread

In the past decade, Krispy Kreme, Inc., became an American success story because of the company's commitment to bake fresh doughnuts early every morning. Rather than selling any stale product, they dispose of it.

Fresh bread is also crucial for Christian development. Morning is the best time for getting to know God. This principle was deeply impressed on the children of Israel through God's gift of manna. It rained down from heaven early in the morning, six days a week. If they waited too long, the manna would evaporate. "So they gathered it every morning, every man according to his need. And when the sun became hot, it melted" (Exodus 16:21).

Likewise, if we wait too long to have our devotions, the cares and pressures of the day will grab our attention before we turn it to the Lord. So, don't let the manna melt! And remember, the busier we are and the more we have to do, the greater our need to take time to study God's Book and pray.

Jesus, our perfect example, followed the practice of having morning devotions. He considered it as essential to life as is physical food—and in some senses, even more important. " 'I have treasured the words of His mouth more than my necessary food' " (Job 23:12). If you are late for work and must choose between your raisin bran or personal devotions, I say that while fiber is important, it will not keep you from sin. "Your words were found, and I ate them, and

Your word was to me the joy and rejoicing of my heart" (Jeremiah 15:16).

The Lord's Prayer contains the line, "Give us this day our daily bread." We should consider that line as applying more to the spiritual bread than the baked variety. When Jesus was tempted in the wilderness after a forty-day fast, He told the devil, " 'It is written, "Man shall not live by bread alone, but by every word of God" ' " (Luke 4:4).

I can't explain it, but it seems that spiritual food gave Jesus not just spiritual strength, but also physical strength. John 4:31, 32, records, "His disciples urged Him, saying, 'Rabbi, eat.' But He said to them, 'I have food to eat of which you do not know.' "

Elijah also received supernatural physical strength from eating heavenly bread that an angel prepared. "The angel of the LORD came back the second time, and touched him, and said, 'Arise and eat, because the journey is too great for you.' So he arose, and ate and drank; and he went in the strength of that food forty days and forty nights as far as Horeb, the mountain of God" (1 Kings 19:7, 8). You might also find that if you wake up a little earlier for more devotional time with God, you will have increased energy throughout the day.

Although we covered some of this in the last section, it bears repeating: If we want to defeat the enemy who is always ready to assail us, we need the same secret weapon Jesus used. It is described aptly in Ephesians 6:17: "Take . . . the sword of the Spirit, which is the word of God."

We all desperately need and want to have Jesus abiding in our hearts. How do we get Him there? Another name for Jesus is "the Word." When we are reading the Word, we are directly inviting Jesus into our hearts and minds. "Your word I have hidden in my heart, that I might not sin against You" (Psalm 119:11).

Since Jesus is the Word, He's also the secret weapon! Again, the principle is that as we spend more time with Jesus through prayer and Bible study, we will know Him better and therefore love Him more. And just as our natural reaction is to talk about those we love, so it will become more natural for us to tell others, both enemy and friend, about our Lord. Then, as we share our faith with others, our faith will become stronger—just as a muscle is strengthened by activity.

More love, more witnessing, better surrender, more energy, even less depression—all this and much more comes in a direct chain reaction that begins when we use the secret weapon of personal devotions. "For the word of God is quick, and powerful, and sharper than any two-edged sword, piercing even to the dividing asunder of soul and spirit, and of the joints and marrow, and is a discerner of the thoughts and intents of the heart" (Hebrews 4:12, KJV).

"If you ask anything in My name, I will do it."
—John 14:14

Jesus Answers Prayer

A man asked Alexander the Great to give him a dowry in exchange for his daughter's hand in marriage. The ruler consented and told him to request of his treasurer whatever he wanted. So he went and asked for an enormous amount.

The treasurer was startled and said he couldn't give him that much without a direct order. Going to Alexander, the treasurer argued that even a small fraction of the money requested would more than serve the purpose. "No," replied Alexander, "Let him have it all. I like that fellow. He does me honor. He treats me like a king and proves by what he asks that he believes me to be rich, powerful, and generous."

Jesus answered the demoniac's unspoken plea for deliverance. He answered the prayers of the Gadara townsfolk when they asked Him to leave. He even answered the "prayers" of the devils when they requested to go into the pigs. It makes me wonder: Why do we pray so little? "Likewise the Spirit also helps in our weaknesses. For we do not know what we should pray for as we ought, but the Spirit Himself makes intercession for us with groanings which cannot be uttered" (Romans 8:26).

One of the best observations about prayer comes from the book *Steps to Christ:*

The darkness of the evil one encloses those who neglect to pray. The whispered temptations of the enemy entice them to sin; and it is all because they do not make use of the privileges that God has given them in the divine appointment of prayer. Why should the sons and daughters of God be reluctant to pray, when prayer is the key in the hand of faith to unlock heaven's storehouse, where are treasured the boundless resources of Omnipotence? Without unceasing prayer and diligent watching we are in danger of growing careless and of deviating from the right path. The adversary seeks continually to obstruct the way to the mercy seat, that we may not by earnest supplication and faith obtain grace and power to resist temptation.*

A fellow who had grown up in the city bought a farm and a milk cow. While in the feed store one day, he complained that his cow had gone dry. "Are you feeding her right?" asked the storeowner.

"I'm feeding her exactly what you've been selling me," said the man.

"Are you milking her at regular times every day?"

"Not exactly. If I only need six or eight ounces of milk for breakfast, I go out and get that and just let her save it up."

Of course, it doesn't work that way. When you're milking cows, you take all that's there or eventually you have nothing. That's true of God's presence too.

---

*Ellen G. White, *Steps to Christ* (Hagerstown, Maryland: Review and Herald, 1908), 94.

We must pray God's Spirit will fill our hearts until they are "overflowing with a good theme" (Psalm 45:1).

*"They . . . found the man from whom
the demons had departed . . . clothed and in his
right mind."—Luke 8:35*

New Clothes

You've probably heard Hans Christian Andersen's fairytale "The Emperor's New Clothes." It's the story of two scoundrels claiming to be gifted tailors who take advantage of a very vain emperor. They say they've invented a method to weave a cloth so light and fine that it looks invisible to all who are too stupid to appreciate its quality.

They eventually present to the emperor what they say is a beautiful garment made of their cloth, which of course he can't see. Not wanting to seem stupid, however, he pretends to admire its fine workmanship and beautiful colors. The scoundrels encourage the emperor to take a ride through the city to show off his stunning new garment. He does, and the people who have heard about the special material compliment the emperor on his new clothes because they don't want to look like fools either. Finally, an honest little boy points out the obvious: "Look! The emperor is naked!"

Just as there is a connection between sitting at Jesus' feet and being in one's right mind, there is an equally strong connection between sitting at His feet and being clothed. " 'Because you say, "I am rich, have become wealthy, and have need of nothing"—and do not know that you are wretched, miserable, poor, blind and naked' " (Revelation 3:17).

We've already discussed the spiritual significance of nakedness, but we might still naturally wonder, "Where did the demoniac get his clothes?"

I think the same One who gave skins to Adam and Eve also took off His robe to cover this naked man's shame. Just as Elijah cast his mantle on the shoulders of Elisha, just as Jacob gave a royal robe to Joseph, just as the father covered his prodigal son's filthy rags, I believe that Jesus covered this man with His own robe.

This image is a symbol for you and me that Jesus will cleanse us from our guilt and shame and cover us with His righteousness. "We are all like an unclean thing, and all our righteousnesses are as filthy rags" (Isaiah 64:6). Only when Jesus gives us His righteousness are we truly in our right mind.

Like blind Bartimaeus, we must rise, throw aside our ragged robes, and come to Jesus (Mark 10:50). An Old Testament prophet uses this very image to picture how God covers our sins: "He . . . spoke to those who stood before Him, saying, 'Take away the filthy garments from him.' And to him He said, 'See, I have removed your iniquity from you, and I will clothe you with rich robes' " (Zechariah 3:4).

⟨⟩

"The whole multitude of the surrounding region of the Gadarenes asked Him to depart from them, for they were seized with great fear. And He got into the boat and returned."—Luke 8:37

Rejecting Jesus

In 1962, the U.S. postal authorities rejected a special Christmas stamp because it suggested a Christian cross. However, the design submitted simply showed a candle, framed by a wreath, burning in a window. There was a concern among hypersensitive critics that people might think the wood in the windowpanes represented a cross. How different from the attitude of the postal authorities seventy years earlier. Then they issued a two-cent stamp that showed Columbus planting a cross in the New World. That stamp was issued October 12, 1892, on the four-hundredth anniversary of the event.

This story accurately depicts an important reality: The world will generally reject the cross and those who bear it. "The message of the cross is foolishness to those who are perishing, but to us who are being saved it is the power of God" (1 Corinthians 1:18).

The cemetery on the dismal shore of Decapolis represents the doomed world, which, on the whole, has rejected Jesus. Like the crowd on the beach who asked Him to leave, like the crowd who rejected Jesus at His trial and cried out for Barabbas, they preferred a lunatic to the Lord. This is profound evidence that they were living under the curse of sin. So, the Savior sailed away. However, he didn't abandon the people because of their rejection. He left a representative to continue to witness to them and to demonstrate how He saves.

Did you notice that it was the ones who had not experienced Jesus who wanted Him to leave and that the one who had felt His power wanted to stay with Him? People who have experienced radical redemption will not ask, "Is church over yet?" Like Mary Magdalene, they will cling to Jesus' feet, and like Jacob, they will embrace the Lord and say, "I will not let You go unless You bless me!" (Genesis 32:26).

The sobering truth is that when someone asks Jesus to leave, He will go. He has manners; He will not force Himself upon anyone. He knocks and calls, but He will not violate our freedom of choice.

Charles Spurgeon made this comment:

When traveling among the Alps, one sees a small black cross planted on a rock or on the brink of a stream or on the verge of the highway to mark the spot where men have met with sudden death by accident. These are solemn reminders of our mortality, but they lead our minds still further. For if the places where men seal themselves for the second death could be thus manifestly indicated, what a scene this world would present! Here the memorial of a soul undone by yielding to a foul temptation, there a conscience seared by the rejection of a final warning, and yonder a heart forever turned into stone by resisting the last tender appeal of love.

As the people of Decapolis began to piece together the day's events, not only of the destruction of the pigs, but also the deliverance of the demoniac, they began to sense that there was One far more awesome, much more to be feared, than the devils that once possessed the now lucid man. I suspect they had dealt with the demoniac on many occasions by chaining him or driving him from their presence, and inexplicably, they chose to treat Jesus in much the same way.

It is ironic that while the demoniac didn't want Jesus to leave the country, the others in that land didn't want Him to stay. It's one of the few times that a miracle drove people away from, rather than closer to, Jesus. It would seem that these people had no Messianic expectations and wanted nothing to do with Someone who had so much awesome power—a power over which they had no control.

As Cary Grant was walking along a street, he met a fellow whose eyes locked onto him with excitement. The man said, "Wait a minute, you're . . . you're—I know who you are! Don't tell me . . . uh, Rock Hud—No, you're . . ."

Grant thought he'd help the struggling fan, so he finished the man's sentence: "Cary Grant."

But the excited fellow said, "No, that's not it! You're . . ."

There was Cary Grant, identifying himself with his own name, but the fellow had someone else in mind.

John says of Jesus, "He was in the world, and the world was made through Him, and the world did not know him" (John 1:10). Even when Jesus identified who He was—the Son of God—the response was not welcome recognition, but rather rejection and crucifixion.

"Behold My hands and My feet, that it is I Myself."
—Luke 24:39
"If anyone desires to come after Me,
let him deny himself, and take up his cross daily,
and follow Me. For whoever desires to save his life
will lose it, but whoever loses his life for My sake
will save it."—Luke 9:23, 24

Scars That Speak, Death That Heals

Adoniram Judson, the renowned missionary to Burma, endured untold hardships while reaching the lost for Christ. For seven heartbreaking years, he suffered hunger and privation. During those years, he was thrown into Ava Prison and for seventeen months was incredibly mistreated. As a result, for the rest of his life, he carried the ugly marks made by the chains and shackles that had cruelly bound him.

Undaunted, upon his release, he asked for permission to enter another province in which he might resume preaching the gospel. The godless ruler indignantly denied his request, saying, "My people are not fools enough to listen to anything a missionary might *say*, but I fear they might be impressed by your *scars* and turn to your religion!"

I suspect that even after Jesus released the demoniac from his chains, he still bore the scars on his limbs from his many years of possession. In one respect, the scars were a testimony to God's grace—just as the scars of Jesus will remind us of His sacrificial love for eternity. The fact that scars linger is also a sobering reminder that while God forgives all our sins, the results of our poor choices might not be reversed in this lifetime.

A few years ago, Karla Faye Tucker became the first woman executed in Texas since the Civil War. While on death row for a gruesome murder, she experienced what appeared to be a complete conversion to Christ. She became a model prisoner and was even forgiven by her victim's family. But she was still given her lethal injection.

We must not miss the fact that accepting Jesus does not always remove the consequences of our sins, nor erase the scars. The results of our sins sometimes last beyond our forgiveness. The salvation Jesus promised to the thief on the cross beside Him was freedom from the ultimate penalty for sin, not from all its temporal consequences. Jesus did not take the thief down off the cross, but He did save him.* In essence, this thief was crucified with Christ.

For the demoniac, the new life of following Jesus began at a tomb.† Paul wrote about this death-rebirth experience: "I have been crucified with Christ; it is no longer I who live, but Christ lives in me; and the life which I now live in the flesh I live by faith in the Son of God, who loved me and gave Himself for me" (Galatians 2:20).

What does it mean to be crucified with Christ?

As a prank, a friend of mine sent me a gift certificate for "One free visit to the infamous Dr. Jack Kevorkian." This is the man who is also known by the morbid moniker "Dr. Death." He's become popular because many people are so tired of hurting that they would rather commit suicide than continue living in pain.

In one sense, a form of suicide is the solution to following Jesus successfully. It's not physical suicide, but ego suicide. Paul wrote, "He who has died has been freed from sin" (Romans 6:7). Dead people don't become offended or lose their tempers. Dead people don't behave selfishly or harbor bitterness and grudges. Dietrich Bonhoeffer observed, "When Christ calls a man, he bids him come and die."

---

* We can thank God that in His mercy He sometimes does alter our circumstances and soften the consequences of our bad choices.

† Mary also ran from a cemetery with new life, rejoicing to share the good news.

Those who are Christ's have crucified the flesh with all its filthy passions and worldly desires. "In the same way, count yourselves dead to sin but alive to God in Christ Jesus" (Romans 6:11, NIV). A. W. Tozer said,

> The man with a cross no longer controls his destiny; he lost control when he picked up his cross. That cross immediately became to him an all-absorbing interest, an overwhelming interference. No matter what he may desire to do, there is but one thing he can do; that is, move on toward the place of crucifixion.

A pastor was showing a fellow minister the brand-new cross his church had sitting atop their steeple. "That cross up there cost us ten thousand dollars," the minister said, glowing.

"Well, then you got cheated," the other minister responded. "There were times when Christians could get them for free."

To a man seeking salvation, Jesus said, "One thing you lack: Go your way, sell whatever you have and give to the poor, and you will have treasure in heaven; and come, take up the cross, and follow me" (Mark 10:21).

"The whole multitude . . . asked Him to depart from them, for they were seized with great fear."
—Luke 8:37

A Storm of Fear

I was amused to read that President Benjamin Harrison and his wife were so afraid of the new-fangled electrical system installed in the White House that they didn't dare touch the switches. If no servants were around to turn off the lights when they went to bed, they slept with the lights on.

In the stories of the crossing of the sea and of the demoniac, everyone except Jesus was entangled in fibers of fear. The disciples were afraid of the storm, only to become afraid of Jesus when He calmed the sea. After Jesus rebuked the storm, He turned and rebuked the disciples for their fear and unbelief. And there was plenty more fear to go around. The disciples were also afraid of the demoniac. The demons were afraid of Jesus. The pig keepers were afraid of the possessed pigs, and the townsfolk were afraid of Jesus.

By calming the raging storm and the raving madman, Jesus demonstrated that He is the Lord of all creation, of both the physical and spiritual worlds. Not only that, His actions brought peace and showed that He has tremendous compassion. What then do so many of us fear?

For several years, John Wesley, the founder of the Methodist church, doubted his own conversion even while he worked tirelessly as a pastor. One day he boarded a ship to cross the Atlantic along with a number of Moravian Christians. En route, they encountered a terrible storm. All hands were on deck as the vessel reeled violently on the dark ocean waves. Wa-

The Divine Deliverance

ter was rushing in, and the sails were ripping; yet these Moravian families stood peacefully on deck, singing hymns.

Wesley, who was clinging, terrified, to the side of the ship, asked, "Aren't you afraid?"

One of the men replied, "No, I'm not afraid."

"Well," asked a perplexed Wesley, "aren't the women and the children afraid?"

The man said, "No, we're not afraid to die. Our lives are in God's hands."

At that point, Wesley became convicted that he didn't really have faith in God. Not long after, the Prince of Peace converted his heart. Later, Wesley wrote, "He that fears God, fears nothing else. If you do not fear God, you fear everything else."

Scripture says, "There is no fear in love; but perfect love casts out fear, because fear involves torment. But he who fears has not been made perfect in love" (1 John 4:18). Christians who have genuine faith trust God regardless of external circumstances. They know they have nothing of which to be afraid, because He's on the throne.

The *Titanic* was built in Belfast, and people of that city took great pride in the mighty vessel that was heralded far and wide as "the unsinkable ship." When she sank, sixteen members of a Protestant church in Belfast, all skilled mechanics, went down with her. The mayor said that the city had never been in such grief as that which came by way of the terrible tragedy. Indeed, so profound was the grief that it is said that when even the most stoic men met upon the streets, they grasped each other's hands, burst into tears, and parted without a word.

On the Sunday after the tragedy, a popular American minister who was visiting Belfast preached in the church to which the sixteen mechanics had belonged. The building was packed with people—not just church members, but also lords, bishops, and ministers of all denominations. The sobbing of many newly made widows and orphans filled the otherwise silent room.

The great preacher took as his subject "The Unsinkable Ship." However, he didn't preach about the eleven-story giant that struck the iceberg. No, his message was about that other "unsinkable ship"—the frail little fishing boat on the Sea of Galilee, unsinkable because the Master was asleep on a pillow in the aft of the vessel. He said:

> Thank God, He [Jesus] still lives and rides the billows and controls the storms, and when the children of men take their only true Pilot back on board, they have nothing to fear. We will ride out the present storms, and He will bring the vessel through to the fair harbor of our hopes.

God hasn't promised to keep us out of storms but, instead, to get us through them. Though the Lord commanded the disciples to cross the sea, He didn't guarantee them a calm passage. Jesus might not prevent a storm from striking at a ship, but He will not let it sink the ship. If Jesus is in the boat, we have nothing to fear. We will reach our destination.

"He brought them out of darkness and the shadow of death, and broke their chains in pieces."
—Psalm 107:14

From Prison to the Palace

In one of history's strangest reversals of fortune, South Africa's Nelson Mandela, who had been imprisoned for more than twenty years by that country's former apartheid government, became its president in 1994 as well as the winner of the 1993 Nobel Peace Prize. Similarly, Bible history is dappled with amazing examples of those who have transitioned from the prison to the palace. The following is one of the most beautiful.

It came to pass in the thirty-seventh year of the captivity of Jehoiachin king of Judah, . . . that Evil-Merodach king of Babylon, in the year that he began to reign, released Jehoiachin king of Judah from prison. He spoke kindly to him, and gave him a more prominent seat than those of the kings who were with him in Babylon. So Jehoiachin changed from his prison garments, and he ate bread regularly before the king all the days of his life" (2 Kings 25:27-29).

BROKEN CHAINS

What a splendid symbol of salvation! The king of Babylon shows mercy to Jehoiachin, who had been languishing in a dungeon for thirty-seven years. He not only frees him from his chains but also speaks tenderly to him and gives him new royal robes in exchange for his prison rags. He even grants him a majestic seat at his own table in the palace in Babylon and feeds him with royal food from the palace kitchen. What's more, he does this for the rest of life—an obvious symbol of the coming eternity.

Jehoiachin's story is also the story of the demoniac's deliverance and the story of our salvation. After we come to Jesus just as we are, He not only breaks our chains and brings us out of our dark prison but also gives us new royal clothing. He changes our status from death-row prisoner to child of the King! "Behold what manner of love the Father has bestowed on us, that we should be called children of God!" (1 John 3:1).

In one day, Joseph's rank was changed from imprisoned slave to the prime minister of Egypt. In one day, Moses' status was changed from doomed helpless baby slave to son of the pharaoh.* Likewise, Daniel's position was changed from Judean captive to chief counselor of Babylon.

---

*In fact, the entire Exodus story is a story of how God breaks the chains of a whole nation and transforms them from slaves to royalty: "You shall be to Me a kingdom of priests and a holy nation" (Exodus 19:6).

God has a royal plan for your life too! This is what He wants to do for you: He wants to grant you freedom from your chains, to give you a new name, to make you His child, to cover you with His royal robe of righteousness, and to feed you forever with the living bread and the fruit from the tree of life (see Revelation 2:7)! "To Him who loved us and washed us from our sins in His own blood, and has made us kings and priests to His God and Father, to Him be glory and dominion forever and ever" (Revelation 1:5, 6).

"He who overcomes, I will make him a pillar in the temple of My God. . . . And I will write on him My new name."—Revelation 3:12

An Identity Crisis

The crime of identity theft is increasing in America. In this crime, someone wrongfully obtains and uses another's personal data for fraud or deception, typically for economic gain. Unlike your fingerprints, your personal data—especially your Social Security number, bank account or credit card number, and telephone calling-card personal identification number (PIN)—can be terribly abused if they fall into the wrong hands, profiting others at your expense. Every day, hundreds of people across the country report funds stolen from their accounts. In the worst cases, criminals completely take over victims' identities, run up vast debts, and commit crimes, leaving the victims with destroyed credit and a criminal record that takes years to correct.

In 1970, in an entirely different form of identity tampering, the federal government established the Federal Witness Protection Program. This program provides a new identity to individuals who give court testimony or serve as witnesses in situations where doing so could endanger their lives—for instance, in cases against organized crime syndicates. In exchange for this valuable testimony, the government gives each witness a completely new identity, furnishing a new name, legal papers, occupation, and home. The government will even create new histories, complete with high school and college diplomas! In some cases, if a witness has a criminal record, it is wiped perfectly clean!

God promises His redeemed, "You shall be called by a new name, which the mouth of the Lord will name" (Isaiah 62:2). God gives His children a new identity in Christ. "To him who overcomes I will give some of the hidden manna to eat. And I will give him a white stone, and on the stone a new name written which no one knows except him who receives it" (Revelation 2:17).

There's no reason for you to be confused about who you are. Your new identity is a grand one, with a real purpose and a real home. "You are a chosen generation, a royal priesthood, a holy nation, His own special people, that you may proclaim the praises of Him who called you out of darkness into His marvelous light" (1 Peter 2:9).

The Divine Deliverance

A naturalist visiting a farm one day was surprised to see a beautiful eagle in the farmer's chicken coop. Befuddled, he asked, "Why in the world is that eagle living with chickens?"

"Well," answered the farmer, "I found an abandoned eagle's egg one day and laid it in the coop, and a chicken adopted it and raised the creature after it hatched. It doesn't know any better; it thinks it's a chicken." The eagle was even pecking at grain and strutting awkwardly in circles.

"Doesn't it ever try to fly out of there?" asked the naturalist, noticing that the bird never lifted its gaze. "No," said the farmer, "I doubt it even knows what it means to fly."

The naturalist asked to take the eagle a few days for experiments, and the farmer agreed. The scientist placed the eagle on a fence and pushed it off, bellowing, "Fly!" But the bird just fell to the ground and started pecking. He then climbed to the top of a hayloft and did the same thing, but the frightened bird just shrieked and fluttered ungraciously to the barnyard, where it resumed its strutting.

Finally, the naturalist took the docile bird away from the environment to which it had grown accustomed, driving to the highest butte in the county. After a lengthy and sweaty climb to the hillcrest with the bird tucked under his arm, he peered over the edge and then spoke gently: "You were born to soar. It is better that you die here today on the rocks below than live the rest of your life being a chicken. It's not what you are."

Then, with its keen eyesight, the confused bird spotted another eagle soaring on the currents high above the bluff, and a yearning was kindled within it. The naturalist threw the majestic beast up and over the edge, crying out, "Fly! Fly! Fly!"

The eagle began to tumble toward the rocks below, but then it opened its seven-foot span of wings and, with a mighty screech, instinctively began to flap them. Soon it was gliding gracefully, climbing in ever-higher spirals on unseen thermals into the blue sky. Eventually, the mighty eagle disappeared into the glare of the morning sun. The bird had become what it was born to be.

"Jesus came and spake unto them, saying, All power is given unto me in heaven and in earth. Go ye therefore, and teach all nations."—Matthew 28:18, 19, KJV

Go and Tell

When Robert Moffat, Scottish missionary to Africa, came back to recruit helpers in his homeland, he was greeted by the fury of a very cold British winter. Arriving at the church where he was to speak, he noted that only a small group had braved the elements to hear his appeal.

Although no one responded to Moffat's call for volunteers for mission service in Africa, the challenge thrilled a young boy who had come to work the bellows of the organ. Deciding that he would follow in the footsteps of this pioneer missionary, he went on to school, obtained a degree in medicine, married Moffat's daughter, Mary, and spent the rest of his life ministering to the unreached tribes of Africa. His name: David Livingstone! God works in mysterious ways to carry out His wise purposes.

Usually, when Jesus made a journey to heal someone, it was at the request of a parent or friend. But in this unique story of the demoniac, Jesus crossed the ocean as if commissioned only by His heavenly Father. He made the perilous journey to transform a madman—whom He cleansed, clothed, and then commissioned. It was a total deliverance, an enormous transformation; the man had a brand-new purpose.

I suspect very few churches would consider sponsoring a missionary to cross a stormy sea to reach just one person. By most church standards, people would have counted this missionary endeavor of Jesus a bleak failure. I can almost hear the indignation of the mission board as they reviewed Jesus' journey. "What? You made that dangerous trip, risking the lives of Your associates, just so You could preach to one deranged, naked man? And then You left after only a few hours?"

Christ's trip underscores the incredible value that God places on a single soul—one whom most people, if honest with themselves, would have deemed worthless. Yet Jesus crossed the vast expanse of the universe to reach just you. Yes. If you were the only one to be saved, He would have made the trip from heaven and died on the cross just for you! "What do you think? If a man has a hundred sheep, and one of them goes astray, does he not leave the ninety-nine and go to the mountains to seek the one that is straying?" (Matthew 18:12).

We learn that the particular focus of this man's testimony was in the region of Decapolis. "He departed and began to proclaim in Decapolis all that Jesus had done for him; and all marveled" (Mark 5:20).

As I mentioned earlier, Decapolis was a federation of ten cities (*deka* means "ten"; *polis* means "city") that lay east of Galilee and the Jordan River. If you had interviewed all the residents of Decapolis and asked them to vote for the most unlikely candidate for conversion, this nameless man would have won the vote unanimously. Yet Jesus crossed a stormy sea to save this one man, and then He made him His first missionary.

That's right! Jesus sent this man out preaching even before He sent the disciples on their first preaching tour. The converted demoniac became Jesus' first missionary. There can be little doubt that his most eloquent testimony was about the radical transformation that Jesus made in his life, proclaiming the great things the Lord had done for him.

In fact, Jesus gives this blessed ministry of witnessing to every saved sinner. We come to Jesus; then we go for Him. The Lord invites us to come to Him in the context of the great invitation: "Come to Me, all you who labor and are heavy laden, and I will give you rest" (Matthew 11:28). Then He bids us go for Him under the mandate of the great commission: "Go therefore and make disciples of all the nations" (Matthew 28:19).

The Lord has sent us to "proclaim liberty to the captives, and the opening of the prison to those who are bound" (Isaiah 61:1). In fact, telling others our testimony of what Jesus has done for us is part of our rehabilitation from bondage. "They overcame him [Satan] by the blood of the Lamb and by the word of their testimony" (Revelation 12:11).

This man was so grateful for his salvation from demon possession and his new life that he wanted to tell everyone. He who is forgiven much, loves much. Mary Magdalene had seven devils cast out of her and then went on to become one of Jesus' most devoted disciples.

Indeed, when the demoniac left on his first mission, he was still filled by a spirit—but now by a radically good Spirit, who was there as an invited guest and not as an invader.

"The man from whom the demons had departed
begged Him that he might be with Him.
But Jesus sent him away, saying, 'Return to your
own house, and tell what great things
God has done for you.' And he went his way
and proclaimed throughout the whole city what great
things Jesus had done for him."—Luke 8:38, 39

Going Home

A young man bound for the mission field found himself seated on an airplane next to Billy Graham. He eagerly told the famed evangelist how he was on his way to some remote mission station, where he confidently expected to lead many heathen to the Lord.

Graham said that was wonderful news. Then he asked how many souls the young missionary had brought to Jesus in his family or neighborhood. Looking a little downcast and distracted, the young man responded that he had not brought anyone to the Lord yet—and then he commenced to offer a series of contrived excuses for why it was so difficult to produce converts in his hometown.

After a prayerful pause, Graham soberly advised the young man to return home, saying, "If you have not been successful in reaching anybody in your family or neighborhood, it is likely you'll not experience success in a foreign land either."

As Jesus began to board the boat to leave Decapolis, the newly restored man pleaded that he might accompany Him. What a transformation! The one who so feared His arrival now dreaded His departure. It is likely that he even wished to become one of the Lord's disciples.

But the commission Jesus gave the demoniac was considerably different from His instructions to others He had healed. Usually, He told them to keep quiet about what He had done for them (see Matthew 8:4; Luke 8:56).* The former demoniac was not to sit at Jesus' feet indefinitely either, but to go and tell others about Jesus—beginning with those in his own home.[†]

So many sit in church week after week and never share their faith. As a result, their Christian experience atrophies. The "home" environment represents the best but also the most challenging training ground for developing missionaries. The first person the disciple Andrew led to Jesus after he found Him was his own brother, Peter (John 1:40, 41). When the Samaritan woman at the well learned Jesus was the Messiah, she immediately went to share the Living Water with her neighbors (John 4:28, 29). Jesus even asked His disciples to begin witnessing to those who were closest at hand and then expand that circle outward—ultimately, to the far corners of the earth. "You shall be witnesses to Me in Jerusalem, and in all Judea and Samaria, and to the end of the earth" (Acts 1:8).

It is also important to note that Jesus did not command the former demoniac to go home and become a great orator, but simply to give testimony to what Jesus had done in his life. Being a witness is as simple as that! It will always be true that there is no more

---

*There were volatile political tensions between the people of Galilee and Judea and their Roman overlords. If Jesus' miracles were too widely publicized, they would have fanned the messianic hopes of the people into flames of revolt. There was no such danger in Decapolis; therefore, the mercy of the Lord was to be freely proclaimed.

†Notice that Jesus first told the demons to go and then He told the man to go. Jesus sent the demons to the pigs, and He sent the man to the lost. It is also symbolic that the ones who took care of the pigs left to share bad news. After the demoniac's encounter with Jesus, he went to the same area to share the good news.

powerful sermon than a life that Jesus has transformed! "He went on his way and proclaimed throughout the whole city what great things Jesus had done for him. So it was, when Jesus returned, that the multitude welcomed Him, for they were all waiting for Him" (Luke 8:39, 40).*

Perhaps you have some dear family members or friends who have drifted far from God. Perhaps they're caught in a downward spiral of self-destruction. You might even wonder if your many prayers in their behalf are a waste of time. The good news is that if Jesus could reach this man, He can reach anybody! No condition other than death itself could ever have appeared more hopeless, no bondage more complete. This man was truly as far from God as we could ever imagine. In other words, there is always hope, so don't ever give up on those you love.

Before we leave this story, please take in this amazing contrast one last time:

The possessed man moves among decomposing carcasses in the shadow of the surrounding hills, snorting the cries of the foul swine. His ripped and raw flesh drags remnants of mangled shackles and chains. Screaming and moaning, his snarling mouth foaming

---

*The Gospel of Luke implies that Jesus returned to this district and that because of the powerful ministry of this one man, the whole region was waiting for Jesus when He returned. That is our job too. Jesus is returning to earth very soon, and we are to do all we can through our word and example to prepare others to meet Him in peace.

with saliva, he wanders aimlessly among the silhouettes of caves and tombs, his stinking, naked body followed by a cloud of flies. He continually stabs at his scarred limbs with dirty rocks, and his wild eyes glare menacingly from under his dirty, matted hair.

Isaiah 1:5, 6, describes this so well: "You will revolt more and more. The whole head is sick, and the whole heart faints. From the sole of the foot even to the head, there is no soundness in it, but wounds and bruises and putrefying sores; they have not been closed or bound up, or soothed with ointment." Before meeting Jesus, the demoniac was the ultimate picture of LOST—all capital letters! He was unclean, unsociable, unrestrained, and tormented.

And now the contrast: After he came to Jesus, he was tranquil, civilized, clothed, smiling, and in his right mind.

What a difference Jesus made in his life! It was the difference between light and darkness, lost and found, and life and death. Jesus can and will make that same difference in your life too! As someone once said, "When I look at myself, I wonder how I can be saved. When I look at Jesus, I wonder how I can be lost." Whatever your chains might be, Jesus can break them and set you free. "If any man be in Christ, he is a new creature: old things are passed away; behold, all things are become new" (2 Corinthians 5:17, KJV).

If you have not already asked Jesus to save you, ask Him to do so now. Then go and tell what great things He has done for you.

Do not let sin reign in your mortal body, that you should obey it in its lusts. And do not present your members as instruments of unrighteousness to sin, but present yourselves to God as being alive from the dead, and your members as instruments of righteousness to God. For sin shall not have dominion over you, for you are not under law but under grace.

What then? Shall we sin because we are not under law but under grace? Certainly not! Do you not know that to whom you present yourselves slaves to obey, you are that one's slaves whom you obey, whether of sin leading to death, or of obedience leading to righteousness? But God be thanked that though you were slaves of sin, yet you obeyed from the heart that form of doctrine to which you were delivered. And having been set free from sin, you became slaves of righteousness (Romans 6:12-18).